THE FRENCH ALTERNATIVE
THE PLEASURE AND COST-EFFECT
OF KEEPING YOUR BOAT IN FRANCE

DAVID JEFFERSON

WATERLINE

Published by Waterline Books
an imprint of Airlife Publishing Ltd
101 Longden Rd, Shrewsbury, England

ISBN 1 85310 298 9

A Sheerstrake production.

A CIP catalogue record of this book
is available from the British Library

Contents

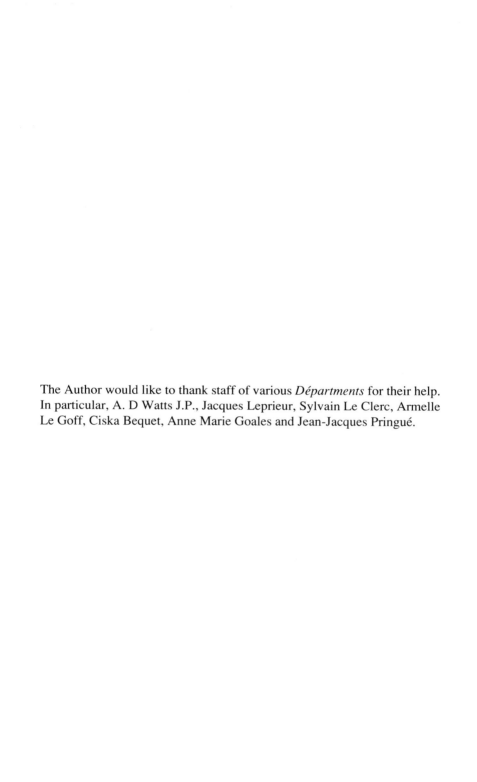

The Author would like to thank staff of various *Départments* for their help. In particular, A. D Watts J.P., Jacques Leprieur, Sylvain Le Clerc, Armelle Le Goff, Ciska Bequet, Anne Marie Goales and Jean-Jacques Pringué.

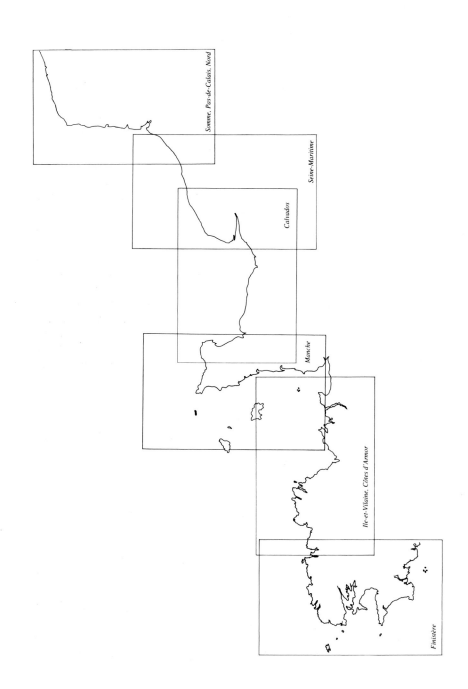

Somme, Pas-de-Calais, Nord

Seine-Maritime

Calvados

Manche

Ille-et-Vilaine, Côtes d'Armor

Finistère

1 The French Alternative

Base your boat across the Channel

Almost every month, we read in one or other of the yachting magazines about the spiralling costs of a marina berth in the UK, particularly in those yacht harbours along the already overcrowded South Coast. One editor warns his readers that if they are contemplating buying a new boat, they should reckon on having to spend an additional 10% of her value in the first year on berthing fees. In subsequent years, this percentage gets depressingly higher with depreciation on the boat and regular increases in mooring charges.

The author suggests an alternative to paying these excessive charges or having to produce a capital sum to lease a berth – a scheme which some property developers have introduced. Why not consider a permanent berth on the French side of the English Channel? (or the Manche as the French call it.) Apart from the UK/France cost comparisons (a persuasive argument in its own right), there are other benefits. For those boat owners who have strictly limited time for cruising, a French base can mean a new and more exciting cruising ground, with plenty of time to explore. How else could the owner of say a 25-footer spend a leisurely annual holiday sailing the boat around the North Biscay yacht harbours and anchorages?

How much will it cost and what are the savings?

A simple example: consider the 1992 charges for keeping a boat in Port Chantereyne (Cherbourg), compared with the cost of a berth in Brighton Marina.

It is very difficult to compare like with like, but Cherbourg and Brighton are similar in some respects. Both are well inside sea walls, and the facilities at each, including yacht clubs, are not all that different. A boat owner crossing the Channel from Brighton, will then be in much the same cruising ground as that available to the owner of a boat based on Cherbourg. One can hardly say that Brighton town is similar to Cherbourg – the former caters for tourists in a big way with extensive beaches and two piers, while the latter is a working commercial port, with a tiny beach and little to attract visitors, apart from those arriving in huge numbers by yacht. Brighton Marina is a private development, and one of only a handful of UK yacht harbours where the operators did not increase the charges for 1992. Cherbourg is a municipal harbour, and values greatly the income to the town generated by Port Chantereyne. Municipal yacht harbours in France can only apply modest increases, with an upper limit dictated by the Government (The 1992 increase was 4%).

The annual charge for a 10m yacht at Brighton is £2250 which also covers water, two car passes, and security. The annual cost at Cherbourg for a 10m yacht is 8,235fr (c £866 in 1992) which includes water and electricity.

Perhaps some may feel that the above is overstating the case, for Cherbourg really does represent astonishingly good value, but then that is true of many of the yacht harbours on the French side of the Manche.

Another interesting comparison might be Newhaven with Port Guillaume, a new private development to the East of Ouistreham. The annual cost at Newhaven for a 10m yacht works out almost the same as Brighton. Newhaven's annual charge includes harbour dues, electricity, water, joint yacht club membership and storage ashore. The 1992 *tarif annuelle* at Port Guillaume is 10,815fr (c £1138) which makes it one of the more expensive of the French Channel yacht harbours (comparable with the private development at fashionable Deauville). Even this comparison reflects a difference of more than £1000 a year. Both Newhaven and Port Guillaume can be used for about 8 hours a tide; Port Guillaume has a single gate to maintain 2.5m in the basin. This development at Dives-sur-Mer opened in 1991, and parts may look like a building site for a year or two, but the surrounding holiday resorts here are delightful.

A third random example might be the Mayflower International marina, at Plymouth, compared with Brest's Moulin Blanc marina. Costing just over £2000 a year, again for a 10m yacht, Mayflower International offer a permanent berth along with use of the yacht club, car parking space and after-hours access to the site by entry card. Brest is a much larger marina, well equipped, but on the outskirts of the town and with no yacht club. The author suggests Brest as an excellent base from which to explore locally or to press on round the Pointe du Raz to the North Biscay ports (see section on Finistère). The 1992 cost of a berth in Port du Moulin Blanc works out at less than £800 a year.

On the West coast of Brittany, the average 1992 cost of a pontoon berth for a 10m yacht in a popular marina is between £6-700, and less for some of the Channel ports. This could represent a saving of around £1,500 a year, compared with what the boat owner is paying for a similar berth in one of the English South Coast marinas.

More detailed cost comparisons are left to the reader. There is a similar saving on the use of a mooring buoy (*corps mort*) as an alternative to a pontoon berth. And this is not the end of the story – a glance at the other costs in French marinas for winter maintenance etc. will come as a pleasant surprise.

So why pay more?

Given the huge savings on annual mooring fees, and the prospect of more leisurely cruising along the French coastline, what are the snags? There are several. Many boat owners will feel that the prime purpose for investing in a boat is to get away from rigid sailing times and long queues associated with crossing the Channel by ferry. It is not quite the same as slipping quietly from the marina berth in the UK, with a good forecast, and then arriving in one's own boat in a favoured yacht harbour on the other side of the Channel.

With a boat conveniently near home in a UK yacht harbour, the boat owner can take advantage of a fine weekend; the season can often be extended by the arrival of an Indian summer. For many, one of the pleasures of owning a boat is to be able to escape from the chores for a few hours on the pretext of having to do some tinkering with the engine. This often provides the opportunity of meeting up with fellow boat owners (who are doing the same thing), and perhaps talking about the plans for next summer's cruise. None of this will be possible if your boat lies wrapped up for the winter across the Channel at Carentan, Le Havre or in the Rade de Brest. Some boat owners will genuinely feel that whatever the financial savings, these will not compensate for the freedom of choice they presently enjoy, and which would have to be surrendered if the boat was miles away in some harbour on the other side of the Channel.

What about those waiting lists?

It would be misleading not to draw the reader's attention to the fact that some of the yacht harbours along the coastline covered by this guide, are now operating waiting lists for permanent berths. These tend to be situated on the West coast of Brittany, where boats can be reached in a couple of hours from Paris. By way of example, there are waiting lists for permanent berths at three of the four Sagemor managed yacht harbours around the Morbihan. Port Haliguen, La Trinité-sur-Mer and Port Crouesty are all full, but there is still space at Arzal-Camoel on the

Vilaine river, just above the Barrage d'Arzal. It is a good marina with pontoon space on both sides of the river, but anyone keeping their boat here would have to have a car or pay hefty taxi fares, for the site of Arzal-Camoel marina is somewhat remote. Having said that, it is just 5 miles downriver from the marina to the Vilaine estuary, beyond which is possibly the finest cruising ground in Brittany, with the entrance to the Morbihan to the North, Belle Ile to the West and Le Croisic and La Baule to the South.

At any of the marinas operating waiting lists for pontoon berths, they may well be able to offer a mooring buoy which may be almost as convenient and considerably cheaper. This arrangement could be tried out for the first season, perhaps wintering ashore and then being able to negotiate a pontoon berth for the following season. There is certainly more space along the North coast (exceptions Granville, St Servan's Port des Bas Sablons, Lézardrieux and Morlaix). What is encouraging is that several of the French marinas already have plans underway to increase the number of pontoon spaces.

Travel to and from the boat.

Anyone opting for the *French Alternative*, will have to adjust to the disciplines of planning summer holidays well in advance. Booking of space for the car on the cross-channel ferries may mean making a reservation in January or even earlier.

The savings achieved will more than pay for several Channel crossings by ferry with a car for boat owner and crew. By way of example, Sealink-Stenna's 'All-in Car' return fare between Southampton and Cherbourg, is around £300 which covers car and up to five passengers (cabin charge extra). P & O European Ferries, sailing between Portsmouth and Cherbourg have an attractive 'Family Bonus' return (two adults, up to three children plus car.)

Portsmouth – St Malo by Brittany Ferries (two adults, two children and car) costs a little over £300 for the return trip. With the competition of EuroTunnel, the ferry companies are coming up with some very attractive special rates, so apart from the annual holiday, the boat owner can take the occasional long weekend or a 5-day break and reach the boat with little outlay.

The point has to be made about early booking of car space on the ferries. This can, however, be qualified. If the boat is based in Cherbourg for example, a car may well be considered unnecessary. If the boat is in Carentan, then from Cherbourg there is a useful train service, many buses, and a taxi will only cost around 50 francs. Part of this guide is devoted to information about public transport in the part of France under review. A reader might be surprised that disembarking from the Portsmouth – St Malo night crossing, it is possible to reach Vannes on the West coast of Brittany in less than three hours by train.

Security and Boat Insurance

This is a difficult one on which to generalise. As in the UK, boats in some French harbours do seem to be more vulnerable to pilfering than in others. If the boat is permanently based across the Channel, your insurance company may well want information relating to the security of the chosen yacht harbour. Has the public free access? Are the pontoons patrolled day and night by security staff? Some boat owners will make their choice of yacht harbour depending on the replies received to these questions. If the boat owner's existing insurance company wants to increase the premium simply because the boat is to be based in France, then obtain a quote from another company that does not base the insurance premium on the location of the boat.

Many boat owners faced with ever more increases for their marina berths on the South coast of England, may already be looking at the small print on their berthing agreements with a view to abandoning their UK harbour for pastures new on the other side of the Channel. The author's view is that the pleasures of cruising along the French coast without the worry of having to get the boat back to the UK, more than offsets the restricted use of the boat. And, let's face it, that trip down to see the boat in winter is only an excuse not to get on with the home decorating.

The next section is a coastline guide for those considering the 'French Alternative'. It is divided up into Départements (the equivalent of our Counties).

2 Channel West

Manche
Carentan – St Vaast-la-Hougue – Barfleur – Cherbourg – Omonville
– Dielette – Carteret – Portbail – Granville.
(plus English and French Channel Islands.)

Cross-channel Port Cherbourg

The Manche Département's seaboard virtually coincides with what is
otherwise known as the Cotentin Peninsula. It is an interesting cruising
ground, much monopolised over the years by visiting British yachts.
Cherbourg, the region's ferry port, offers a highly competitive annual
tariff to boat owners looking for a permanent berth in Port Chantereyne.
The facilities here are excellent, and craft can be left for several weeks
in a yacht harbour that is regularly patrolled by security staff. Crews of
yachts based here have a useful choice of cross-channel ferry services
(Portsmouth, Southampton, Poole).

To the East of Cherbourg is Barfleur, a drying fishing harbour, with a
rock-encumbered entrance. For years there have been plans to develop
Barfleur by building a yacht harbour here. All these plans have
eventually come to nothing, perhaps to the satisfaction of those few boat
owners who relish piloting along the approach channel and whose boats
are suitable either for taking the ground in the middle of the harbour or
drying out alongside the quay. Now, at last, there is a scheme which
might eventually see the light of day. Barfleur will then become, for
many visiting yachts, an alternative to Cherbourg for the long weekend.
For some years, St-Vaast-la-Hougue has taken on this role, being less
crowded than Cherbourg, and still managing to retain some of its fishing
port characteristics.

14 miles below St-Vaast is the entrance channel to Carentan, which is
just inside the Départemental boundary, separating the Manche harbours
from those of the Calvados. Carentan is interesting because this was the
first of the Channel yacht harbours to seize the opportunity of
encouraging English boat owners to base their boats in their yacht
harbour. This is safely tucked away in a canal, 8 miles from the most
seaward buoy of the Chenal de Carentan. They can rightly claim to be
the crème de la crème of the French Channel harbours, regularly picking
up the European Blue Flag award for the high standard of their marina

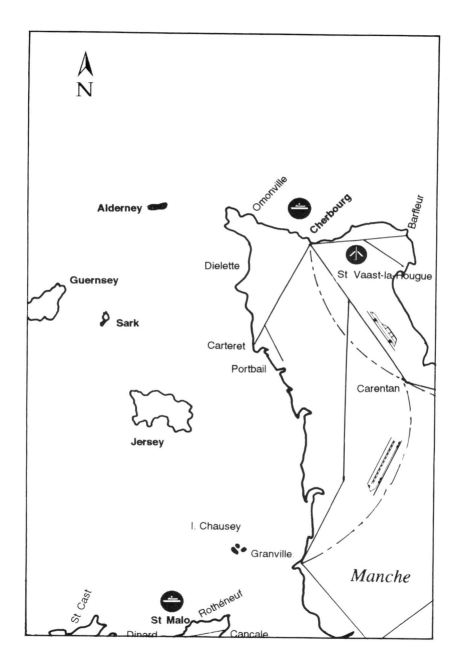

facilities. Carentan advertises amazingly low costs for a permanent berth for English boat owners when compared with the cost of a similar berth along England's South coast.

To the West of Cherbourg is the popular small yacht harbour at Omonville, and an anchorage off the minute Port Racine. Then comes Cap de la Hague, with Alderney just 8 miles further West, and with the infamous Alderney Race between them. In considering the advantages of basing a boat on or close to Cherbourg, one cannot omit the Channel Islands which, given the right conditions, are all just a single tide away from the yacht's home port. Anyone keeping their boat at Cherbourg, St-Vaast or Carentan, may well want to include the Channel Islands on the itinerary of a summer's cruise or even a long weekend.

The harbours on the West coast of the Manche Département are not much visited by English yachts, except for Granville which has a large Port de Plaisance. Between Cap de la Hague and Granville are four harbours – Goury, Dielette, Carteret and Portbail. All four dry, and have entrances exposed to the prevailing winds. This coastline may become more popular with the completion of a remarkable long-term project at Dielette to provide a well-protected deep water harbour.

Lastly, this summary of the Manche harbours and anchorages, would be incomplete without a mention of the islands of Chausey (off the West coast) and St Marcouf (to the East).

Cherbourg

It is hardly surprising that over the years, the vast majority of yachts visiting Cherbourg have been British (nearly 70% in 1991). It is not just the attraction of bonded-stores that draws so many to Cherbourg or the vast hypermarkets with their amazing prices for bottled Alsace beer, wine, and much more besides.

For many boat crews, Cherbourg marks the end of their first Channel crossing. It is easy to approach, the one qualification being the cross-tide which reaches a maximum of 4 knots at springs, so a yacht has to be on the correct side of Cherbourg to approach the port with the tide; this avoids the penalty of having to stay out at sea for a few more hours.

Years ago, the handful of British yachts who did make for Cherbourg would secure to one of a single line of visitors' buoys provided in the Avant Port. A short bow line was attached to the buoy, running a longer stern line ashore so that the boat could rise and fall with the tide. It was only possible to land here using the yacht's dinghy, and at low water this involved something of a scramble to reach the top of the only gangway.

What looked like a small prefab on the quayside, was Cherbourg's yacht club. Inside, the place was invariably filled by the British. There was an air of camaraderie, as many of the crews already knew each other. There was a favoured restaurant too, where the coat stand would be creaking under the weight of oilskin jackets.

Henri Ryst, the original supplier of bonded stores, had an office overlooking the Quai de l'ancien Arsenal. You could purchase a bottle of Gordon's Export Gin for 50p. Standing in the small room looking disbelievingly at the price list, yacht crews would then order an almost limitless quantity of spirits, wine and tobacco. This was brought to the quayside a few hours later, under the strict supervision of both Douanes and Gendarmes. Nowadays bonded-stores are available from *Cherbourg General Yachting* at Port Chantereyne or from *J & C Gruen* in the town.

How different the place is today. Around 10,000 yachts (representing about 30,000 additional visitors) were recorded in Cherbourg in 1991. To cope with this summer invasion, Port Chantereyne increased the number of places from 800 to 1200, making this one of the largest yacht harbours in Normandy. The clubhouse/restaurant is on the first floor of a large building which also contains the yacht harbour offices and a shower block. The town itself has not changed a great deal. It has always been a working port, and at one time the *QEII* berthed here. Now it takes an increasing number of car ferries, so the majority of tourists who land here, drive off almost immediately, bound for Brittany or the South of France.

Many of the visiting yacht crews, will get no further than the yacht club which opens Tuesday – Sunday, 10am to midnight. It is a walk of about ten minutes into the town centre, where there is a market on Thursdays, off Place Divette. For basic groceries and chandlery, there are shops within the Chantereyne complex. There are two hypermarchés on the outskirts of the town; if loading up with supplies for a cruise that starts from Cherbourg, then a taxi back to the port will be necessary.

In this essentially industrial town, there are few concessions to tourism. Children may like the stretches of sand that might just pass for beaches. A swimming pool (piscine) and a sports complex, which includes an ice rink and bowling, are close to the moorings. In the town there is a theatre and, nearer to the docks, a casino.

Barfleur

Barfleur

To some boat owners, Barfleur, 15 miles to the East of Cherbourg, represents nothing more than the end of a smudge of land or a light which remains stubbornly on the same bearing. If the navigator is going to make a mistake in the course to Cherbourg from say the Solent, invariably this means finishing up too far to the East, with the tide making to the East. The penalty is having to spend a few more hours at sea, standing off Barfleur. On a small-scale Admiralty chart, the Barfleur entrance looks intimidating; using a larger-scale, either from one of the Pilots or the inset plan on Imray's chart C.32, the entrance is seen to be well-marked with a useful transit. Three miles to the East and North-East of Barfleur, there is a race to be avoided when the tide is flooding, (tides are weaker inshore). Barfleur itself must be given a miss in a strong NE wind, when the harbour will get distinctly uncomfortable. The entire harbour dries, but the bottom is firm and there may be a space alongside the town quay.

Barfleur is still very much a fishing harbour, and it is good to see that the development plan here makes provision for the fishing fleet. The first stage is to dredge a channel (min 2m) from the deep water off Barfleur, right up to the far end of the old drying harbour. The Capitainerie will be built here, along with a pontoon to take about 30 boats. The second stage is to build a lock and create a *bassin-à-flot* in what is now low marshland. The existing road bridge will be replaced with a lifting bridge. With the completion of this long-term development, the new yacht basin will have a capacity for 650 boats.

St-Vaast-la-Hougue

For some years now, St-Vaast-la-Hougue, has established itself as an alternative to Cherbourg for boat rallies from English South Coast clubs and for long weekends. The yacht basin here (access 2¼ hours before HW to 3 hours after), was built in 1983. Prior to this development, visiting yachts had to make do with a berth in the mud alongside the town quay which they shared with a large fleet of fishing boats.

The entry to St-Vaast is straightforward, leaving Ile de Tatihou to starboard and Fort de la Hougue to port. The fair weather anchorage, just under a mile off, is convenient if waiting for sufficient water to lock in. Ashore there are walks along the causeway to the Vauban fortress, with views across to Utah Beach which is the most Westerly of the D-Day beaches. At low water it is possible to reach Ile de Tatihou on foot. The fishing boats are still at St-Vaast, racing through the lock at the last moment to a berth on the town quay.

There are 150 places for visitors at St-Vaast. The yacht basin is never too full for anyone to be turned away, attracting around 5000 visiting yachts in 1991. Many oysters are landed here, and the fish restaurants, overlooking the harbour, have a good reputation for seafood. Meals are also available at the yacht club. Cherbourg is about 30km from St-Vaast, so anyone travelling by ferry will have to take a taxi (fare approx £15) to or from the boat.

Bonded-stores are available here. First go to the supermarket 'Gosselin' (500m from the pontoons) where they will direct you across the road to their duty-free shop. Bonded-stores are then delivered to the yacht harbour in an unmistakable red vintage van. 'Gosselin' also has one of the finest wine cellars in the region.

Iles St Marcouf

Seven miles South-East of St-Vaast are the Iles St Marcouf – two minute islands that one might miss on the chart except that there is a light here and a South cardinal beacon. On one of the islands (Ile du Large) there is a crumbling Vauban fortress which has its own miniature harbour, where old cannon implanted into the quay still serve as bollards. The author stayed here overnight many years ago, when the entrance to the harbour formed a sill maintaining 4ft of water. Nowadays, St Marcouf's harbour has silted up, and only receives the tenders of yachts in the anchorage between the islands. Landing is prohibited on Ile de Terre, which is a bird sanctuary.

The Iles St Marcouf are just 3 miles off Utah Beach. Three weeks before the D-Day landings, no-one had given a thought to these tiny rocky outposts. In the final count-down to D-Day, staff at the Allied headquarters realised their blunder. With no intelligence information, they decided that the islands could be a site for heavy gun batteries which could massacre the American units about to attempt their planned landings on Utah beach. 132 men of the U.S. assault squadrons were chosen to make an early morning raid on the Marcoufs, 24 hours before the main assault. All was deserted, with no signs of occupation and no heavy guns. But the islands had been mined with a particularly hideous type of explosive. There were many casualties in what turned out to be the first of the thousands of troops who took part in the D-Day Normandy landings.

At the South-East end of Utah beach is a great drying bay, which has two marked channels over the sands; both can only be used with sufficient rise of tide. One channel leads to Carentan, the other to Isigny. Carentan is in the Manche Département, Isigny is in Calvados.

Carentan

Carentan is the home port of a growing number of English boats, defecting from the English South Coast because of the ever increasing costs and the overcrowding.

The first mark of the drying buoyed Chenal de Carentan is one mile off the nearest coastline and 6 miles from the Carentan canal lock. The best time to cross the sands is HW -1½. The lock at Carentan operates HW -2 to HW +3. Between the sea and the lock is featureless

Iles St Marcouf

marshland known as le Marais. After the lock, there is another mile of canal to Carentan's yacht basin.

Carentan has all the usual yacht harbour facilities, including a yacht club. For four successive years, the yacht harbour has won the Blue European flag for the high standards maintained there. Most of the pontoons are on the East side of the canal, and it can be quicker to row across to the West side to visit the town. There is any amount of space for expansion here, and for the boat owner looking for a base in a French Channel port, Carentan does have the advantage over neighbouring St-Vaast; it is linked by rail to the ferry ports of Cherbourg and Caen. There is also a regular bus service to and from Cherbourg.

The Mayor and the local Chambre de Commerce have been particularly active in their attempts to draw visitors to Carentan. The development of the yacht harbour was an exclusively local enterprise. More attractions have now been established here, including a golf driving range, an equestrian centre, a water sports park, a swimming pool and an exercise track.

Omonville

Omonville

The land to the West of Cherbourg is high ground, with little in the way of anchorages except for Omonville. Popular with the British, this anchorage is 10 miles from Port Chantereyne. It is in a bay with a sea wall providing some protection from the North. It is a place to be avoided if there is even a hint of winds from the North-East. Several visitors' buoys have been put down here, and it is also possible to dry out alongside the inner part of the sea wall, close to the beach. There are few facilities ashore, apart from the popular restaurant. It is about 4km to the nearest village.

Port Racine

Another interesting place to visit, 4 miles to the West of Omonville, is Port Racine. This man-made miniature drying harbour is used by a few small fishing boats whose mooring lines bar the way in for any other craft. Given the right conditions, there is a reasonable anchorage in the Anse de St Martin, and one can enter the harbour in a dinghy if, for no other reason, to say that you have been into the smallest harbour in France (the notice here says so!). There is a restaurant a short walk up the hill from the harbour.

Port Racine

The Channel Islands

Although this chapter deals with the Manche harbours, it is appropriate to include more than a passing reference to the Channel Islands (or Iles Anglo-Normandes as the French call them).

Some yachts leaving Cherbourg to cruise westwards will make for Alderney; others will time the passage from Cherbourg to arrive off Cap de la Hague at slack water, and then take the tide to Sark, Guernsey or Jersey.

Alderney

Braye, Alderney's deep water harbour, is 24 miles from Cherbourg's marina. When making this passage in poor visibility, the temptation may be to hug the land, sailing close to Cap de la Hague. If the South-going tide has started in the Alderney Race, then it may well prove impossible to make Braye; irrespective of the set compass course, the tidal stream will have the effect of sweeping a yacht caught this way southwards in the direction of Jersey. As one wit put it, the only way to sail from Cherbourg to Alderney is via Poole!

Visiting yachts are well catered for in Braye harbour. There are 80 visitors' buoys which greatly outnumber the moorings for local boats. These visitors' buoys run down almost the full length of the harbour, close to the breakwater. More buoys are in the centre of the bay and off Fort Albert. Over a fine weekend, these visitors' buoys may have to accommodate 200 plus boats. A visiting yacht will almost certainly have to share a buoy, rafting up alongside. This is all fine and chummy in the prevailing winds, but introduce a North or North-Easterly, and there can be havoc on the buoys. The only remedy is to give Alderney a miss if the forecast is for North or North-Easterlies. A boat based at Cherbourg should have plenty of other opportunities of visiting the island in the prevailing winds (SW), when Braye provides perfect protection.

Although Braye itself is nothing more than a small village, the facilities ashore here are particularly popular with visiting yacht crews. The hospitable sailing club, overlooking the harbour, has a bar and occasionally serves meals. There is an excellent chandler/mechanic (*Mainbrayce*) by the drying inner harbour. Fuel is available alongside between -2½ + 2½ HW. *Mainbrayce* also provide the useful water taxi service to and from the moorings (contactable on Channels 80 or 37 up to midnight).

Guernsey

About 8 miles long by 4 miles wide, Guernsey has a huge influx of summer visitors, many of whom arrive at St Peter Port on the Ro-Ro ferries from Poole. Those who arrive by yacht, will not be disappointed. The situation at St Peter Port, has greatly improved with the completion of the Queen Elizabeth II Marina just North of the harbour. This marina and Albert Marina on the South side of the harbour, are for local boats only, but all the space in Victoria Marina is now available to visiting yachts. There is a visitors' holding pontoon if waiting for a berth in Victoria Marina.

Most yacht crews find St Peter Port particularly attractive. It is only a few minutes walk to the centre of the town. The Royal Channel Islands Yacht Club, available to members of other recognised yacht clubs, overlooks the harbour, and its popularity can be gauged from the visitors' book which you sign when you arrive; more hospitality and very reasonable lunch and supper menus are available at Guernsey Yacht Club, close to Castle Cornet.

Because of memories of the erstwhile overcrowding at St Peter Port, some boat owners still prefer Beaucette Marina, which is in a remote part of the island at Vale on the North-East tip. Although much smaller than Victoria Marina, it is very rare for anyone to be turned away from Beaucette, although larger craft should warn the harbour office here of their intended arrival (VHF Channels 37 and 80). Originally three disused quarries, this yacht harbour was created by dynamiting a gap in the rock face to let the sea in. The entrance is about 18m wide, but as the tide drops the gap shrinks to a mere 8m at half-tide.

There are several fair weather anchorages around the island in attractive sandy bays. Below St Peter Port are Havelet Bay and Fermain Bay, both protected from South-Westerlies. On the island's South coast, and well protected from North or North-East winds, are Petit Port, Moulin Huet Bay , Saints Bay and Petit Bot Bay.

Herm

Just three miles across the water from St Peter Port is Herm and the privately-owned Jethou, with the Passe Percée between the two. Herm attracts a stream of *vedettes*, packed with tourists for a day out on the island. Although only a mile long, Herm has a little drying harbour, a hotel, restaurant, tavern, tea garden, and a tiny shopping piazza.

The anchorage is off the Rosiére Steps, where the *vedettes* berth to land and pick up visitors. Alternatively yachts can dry out in the tiny harbour (usually filled to capacity) or secure to the chains on the beach near the harbour. The other anchorage, protected from South-Westerlies, is off the East side of the island in Belvoir Bay. If the weather is settled, there is something very pleasing about spending the evening on Herm, when all the boat-trippers have returned to St Peter Port. The author has found Herm a convenient stopping-off place if waiting for the tide whilst returning to Alderney or Cherbourg.

The easiest approach to Herm from St Peter Port, and used by the local boats, is the Godfrey Pass which meets up with the Passe Percée. Having landed at Rosiére, there is then the obligatory walk across the island to Shell Beach to bathe and to join the rest of the visitors, walking with their heads bowed down looking for exotic shells to take home as souvenirs.

Sark

For the visiting yacht, the approach to Sark can present something of a challenge. There are isolated rocks all round the island, and overfalls in the approaches to the East side of the island. The pilots refer to tidal races of 7 knots. It is, therefore, a question of picking a period of settled weather, preferably around neaps. If a yacht happens to be in the vicinity in the right conditions, Sark is a must and yacht crews will not be disappointed.

There are anchorages all around the main island (excluding Little Sark). Some are large sandy bays, from which it can be a hard climb to the civilisation in the centre of the island. The *vedettes* from St Peter Port, depending on the direction of the wind, either use the Maseline quay on the East side or Havre Gosselin on the West side. The island's drying harbour, Creux, is on the East side, next to Maseline Harbour. Creux is small (taking a dozen or so boats than can safely dry out), and surrounded by cliffs through which a tunnel has been built for access to the lane leading up to the centre of the island.

The privately-owned island of Brecqhou is separated from the cliffs of Sark's West coastline by the Gouliot Passage, where the tide can hurtle through at 10 knots. Taken in the right conditions, this deep water pass provides an exhilarating experience, and it is possible to sail through although the cliffs on either side mostly blanket the wind.

Immediately South of the Gouliot is the popular anchorage of Havre Gosselin. There is a landing place here, and then a long climb up the stone steps to the top of the cliffs to visit the centre of the island. Other popular anchorages on the East side are Dixcart and Derrible Bays.

Jersey

Jersey handles even more visitors than Guernsey. The island is larger (9 miles long by 6 miles wide) and has a superb 3-mile long beach in St. Ouen's Bay.

Visiting yacht owners have a varied choice of anchorages, although the majority will make their night stopover in the fine marina at St Helier. Access to the marina is over a sill which can be crossed 3 hours either side of high water. The old yacht basin (la Collette), accessible at all states of the tide, now forms a waiting area for yachts intending to berth in St Helier marina. It is only a few minutes walk into the town centre, although the marina itself has all facilities including a shop for provisions. St Helier Yacht Club, near the South Pier and overlooking the entrance to the port, welcomes visitors.

The other Jersey harbour on the South coast is St Aubin which dries to almost a mile offshore. There are some deep water moorings, but it is a long row ashore. The headquarters of the Royal Channel Islands Yacht Club overlooks the harbour at St Aubin. Off the South East of the island are dangerous rocks and shoals that extend almost 8 miles offshore – no place to get caught in strong onshore winds.

Off the island's East coast, is the drying harbour of Gorey (there are some deep water moorings to seaward of the harbour wall). Nothing like the size of St Helier, Gorey always seems packed with visitors – the local attractions being the harbour and Mont Orgueil Castle. The facilities for visiting yachts are good with a yacht club, fuelling from the jetty, boatyard and chandler, with any amount of restaurants, pubs and shops. North of Gorey, at St Catherine's, is a deep water anchorage behind a long breakwater that extends half a mile out to sea at Verclut. On Jersey's North coast are 3 bays – Rozel, Bouley, and Bonne Nuit. This coastline should not be approached in winds between West and East thro' North. If the conditions are settled, the bays here provide delightful day-time anchorages. Rozel has its own fishing harbour which is small and dries. Bouley has a deep water anchorage off the jetty, and Bonne Nuit is a small drying harbour. All three have shops, restaurants and pubs ashore.

Continuing West and rounding Grosnez Point, is St Ouen's Bay, with a beach that belongs to sun worshippers and sand yachts. From Bonne Nuit Bay, a West-bound yacht has to sail halfway round Jersey to reach the next anchorage off St Aubin or the only deep water port at St Helier.

Les Ecréhous

This quick tour of the Channel Islands would be incomplete without a mention of two rocky outposts. Les Ecréhous, a collection of tiny islands and reefs, is 6 miles North East of Gorey, Jersey. Navigation around Les Ecréhous is only possible during daylight hours and can be tricky, particularly at springs, when the tide rips between the rocks around which the boat has to be piloted.

Three of the tiny islands have cottages on them, mostly used in the summer months by owners of Jersey yachts. Maître Ile, the largest of the group (about 600m long), has the remains of a small chapel that belonged to the Abbey of Val Richer. The Abbot was given Maître Ile on condition that the monks kept a beacon burning to warn shipping.

Marmotière, to the North of Maître Ile, is the most spectacular. It has a cluster of a dozen minute stone cottages, some dating back to the 17th century. There are one or two private moorings in the deep water off Marmotière, but anyone planning to stay more than a few hours here or possibly spend the night, should, when there is water, enter the 'pool'. This is half a cable West-South-West of Marmotière where there are more privately owned moorings. At low water springs there is only 1m of water here, but over neaps there is around 1.8m. The anchorage is well protected except in North-Westerlies. As the tide drops, more and more of the Ecréhous are revealed, and Marmotière is connected by a shingle beach to Blanche Ile, the only other island with a few more cottages.

The Minquiers

The other group of rocks and islands with ever-changing views as the tide drops away, is the Minquiers (or Minkies as they are known in the Channel Islands). At low water, the Minquiers is said to cover an area of about 80 square miles. The main island, Maîtresse Ile, is about 10 miles South of Jersey's South coast.

Navigation amongst the Minquiers is tricky at the best of times, and some of the locals say it should be positively discouraged, unless a local can be persuaded to join the crew. There is a neaps anchorage off Maîtresse Ile in about 4m (but virtually dries at springs). The way into the anchorage involves navigating in strong tides, setting a compass course when some distance off, and then following four transit marks.

A yacht sailing westwards, from say Cherbourg, will invariably make for Alderney or round the Cap de la Hague to take the Alderney Race to the other Channel islands. There is in fact, a not-much-used third choice. This is to round smartly Cap de la Hague, and then make for one of the small drying harbours on this West coast of the Cotentin peninsula or press on for Granville. Timing is still all-important, because once round Cap de la Hague, the temptation may be to remain about 2 miles off, where the Alderney Race runs at its strongest (the SSW stream attaining over 7 knots at springs). This side of the Cotentin peninsula is long, wide beaches, flanked by sand dunes, with many offlying dangers. Except around slack water, the approach to the drying harbours between Cap de la Hague and Granville can be tricky. Early identification some way off is essential, so that allowance can be made for any sideways drag of the Alderney Race.

Goury

The first of these drying harbours is Goury, just ½ a mile South-East of Cap de la Hague. This is a tiny harbour with a difficult approach. It is listed in Michelin mainly because of its unique lifeboat station. This is an octagonal building on a turn-table, so that the lifeboat can use one of two launching ramps, depending on the state of the tide. A small ferry service operates between Goury and Alderney and Guernsey.

Dielette

The next drying port, 11 miles South of Cap de la Hague, is Dielette with an easier approach compared to Goury, using a transit of the head of the breakwater of the new harbour, lined up with the end of the breakwater of the tiny Vieux Port. There are plans for an ambitious development at Dielette which would provide a 350-berth Port de Plaisance, accessible at any state of the tide. The plan involves dredging a channel from some way off the outer breakwater, through the outer harbour and into the Vieux Port, which is to be dredged in its entirety.

At present, the entrance to Dielette is about a half cable wide, between the end of the breakwater and the Rochers du Nord. A new breakwater is planned to be built over these rocks. Behind this breakwater more dredging will take place to extend the Port de Plaisance and to provide a Gare Maritime (to take the Dielette-Sark-Guernsey *vedettes*). A new quay will also be provided for the fishing fleet. And the plan goes further – with a lake to the East of the harbour which will be used for water sports and a sailing school.

The development at Dielette was first considered early in '91 when the combined local *Chambres de Commerce* commissioned a study of the outline plan. This study should be completed by Spring 1993. The engineering company, who gained expertise in clearing rocks to open up St-Vaast, has been consulted. Inevitably, in such a hugely expensive project, the port plans will be linked to the building of new apartment blocks overlooking the harbour. These will retain the style of the existing buildings. It is hoped that by March 1995 a new Port de Plaisance and a new community will have been created. The local authorities anticipate that the curiously large number of visitors that come to tour the nearby Flamanville nuclear power station, will also drive down to look at the boating activity in the new port of Dielette.

Until that time, boats that can dry out will continue to use the outer harbour. Dielette itself is little more than a holiday village with a few hotels and shops.

Carteret and Portbail

The next two ports along the coastline – Carteret and Portbail – show no signs of any development. Both ports can only be entered with sufficient rise of tide over the offlying sandbanks and shoals, which must be avoided in onshore winds. Both have neat rows of mooring buoys at the top end of drying inlets. These drying 'yacht harbours', give the impression that they were once planned as deep water marinas, but the money ran out for the almost continuous dredging that would have been required to maintain deep water channels. Care must be taken not to get neaped at Carteret.

Both Carteret and Portbail have landing jetties for the *vedettes* that sail to and from Jersey. Of the two, Carteret is more lively, being a popular holiday resort. There is a pleasant hotel/restaurant by the water and near to the moorings. Plenty of shops and more restaurants line the quayside, which is used by a small fleet of fishing boats. Port Bail, on the other hand, is somewhat bleak. The drying moorings are tucked away amongst high sand dunes. Near the jetty, used by the Jersey *vedette*, is the ferry office, and a small bar that only opens in the high season. For a meal and the shops, it is a mile walk along the causeway to the village of Portbail.

Granville

Granville

The exception in this string of harbours along the Manche's West coast is Granville. Years ago, this important commercial and fishing harbour consisted of a large drying Avant Port and a *bassin-à-flot* with huge lock gates to cope with the exceptionally great range of tide here. In 1975 the yacht harbour, Port Herel, was opened. This was built to the West of the commercial port in an area that was once oyster beds. The water level in the Port de Plaisance is maintained by means of a sill with a lifting gate which allows entry approximately 2½ hours before High Water and 3½ hours after. When there is 0.6m of water above the 6m sill, the gate is lowered and there will be 1.4m between the entrance columns. On the ebb, when the level drops to 1.4m above the sill, the gate is raised. Within the yacht harbour, an illuminated panel displays the water level over the sill, and there is a repeater which is visible from le Loup beacon. The area between le Loup and the marina entrance dries.

In 1981, the Port du Herel was enlarged, increasing the pontoon berths to 1000, of which 150 are reserved for visiting yachts. The excellent facilities include a yacht club which organises a busy yacht racing calendar. Of all the Manche harbours visited in 1991, Granville was the only one for which there was a long waiting list for permanent berths. Perhaps this is not so surprising, as Granville has good road and rail connections, and is well placed for short cruises to the Chausey Islands or Jersey or longer passages to Brittany's *Côte de Granit Rose.*

In the holiday season, Granville attracts many visitors. The town has a reasonable beach, and there are regular boat trips to the Iles Chausey. The fortified Haute-Ville or Upper Town, on the Pointe du Roc, has seen many skirmishes between the French and the English. The town was actually occupied for three years by the British as a base from which to plunder French shipping and execute raids on Mont St Michel. It is a fair climb up to the ramparts of the Haute-Ville, where there are many old buildings including the fortifications of La Grande Porte which now houses a museum. The Upper Town is dominated by the massive granite Eglise Notre-Dame, parts of which date back to the 15th century. The Basse-Ville (lower town) is Granville's shopping centre where there are many hotels and restaurants. On the North side of the peninsula is a casino which overlooks the beach.

Iles Chausey

The Granville Yacht Club has provided a large number of visitors' moorings in the Chausey Sound, which is 9 miles to the West of Port Herel. The Iles Chausey form an archipelago of a reputed 365 islands. Grande Ile is the only populated island. Some of the remainder have bird sanctuaries for rare species, and landing is positively discouraged. There is some similarity to the Minquiers, except that this is French territory and the approach from the South presents no problems; it is simply a matter of rounding the lighthouse on the Southern point of Grande Ile. From there, to the visitors' moorings, the limit of the deep water in the Chausey Sound is well marked. Granville Yacht Club emphasise the importance of using two buoys, mooring fore and aft. Over a fine weekend during the season, it may well be necessary to raft up three or four deep on the buoys.

The Sound is well protected except in fresh North-Westerlies or South-Easterlies, when a combination of wind against tide makes the moorings uncomfortable. There is a landing slipway and a jetty (for the Granville *vedettes*) on Grande Ile, which also has a church, hotel, one or two shops, a post office, a farmhouse and a Château. The Chausey Sound is a popular stopping off place for yachts on passage between Guernsey and St Malo, staying here until the tide is fair.

Chausey Sound

This is almost the extent of the Manche coastline, except for Mont St Michel, which just comes within the Départemental boundary and is therefore Normandy. The Mont is a great tourist draw and visitors in their thousands make for this islet, reached by a causeway. It consists of an abbey and a fortress, standing out as a landmark in every direction except off Granville where, close inshore, it is obscured by the Pointe de Champeaux. Behind the abbey is the 'town', which consists of tightly packed houses either side of narrow passages normally packed solid with visitors. One of these buildings contains a museum. The ground floors of the other houses are souvenir shops and bars.

It would be interesting to know the ratio of visiting cars and buses to visiting boats at Mont St Michel. It must be one boat crew to several thousands of land visitors. The pilots hardly sound encouraging, with references to the drying sands that extend about 8 miles out from the Mont. These sands are covered by tides that are said to come in at the speed of galloping horses. Then there is a reference to the quicksands, which are reputed to have claimed a number of boats. There is in fact an area close to the Mont where craft can dry out on firm sand. If contemplating taking a boat there, it might be wise to join the throngs of visitors for an advance recce. Alternatively, find a local boat to guide you in.

31

Ile-et-Vilaine, Côtes d'Armor
Cancale – Rothéneuf – St Malo – St Servan – Dinard – Dinan – St
Cast – Erquy – Dahouet – St Brieuc – Binic – St Quay-Portrieux –
Paimpol – Ile de Bréhat – Lézardrieux – Pontrieux – Tréguier –
Port-Blanc – Perros-Guirec – Ploumanach – Trébeurden – Lannion

---

Cross-channel Port: St Malo

St Malo

The author has some difficulty in not seeming to be too biased towards
St Malo. Over the years, the family has made use of the Bassin Vauban
for extended stays on several occasions. There are arguments against
basing a boat on St Malo. Firstly, the basin is very much open to the
public; secondly St Malo makes no provision for laying up craft out of
the water at the end of the season. This winter work can, however, be
undertaken at neighbouring St Servan's Port de Plaisance des Bas-
Sablons, or there are several boatyards on the tidal Rance above the
barrage. There is a lack of security in St. Malo's Bassin Vauban, so boat
owners need to take extra precautions to make their craft secure,
removing all the valuables if the boat is left unattended for any length of
time. These two qualifications should not deter boat owners from
considering St Malo as a permanent base for the boat.

The view from the ferry approaching St Malo can hardly fail to
impress. The old town, with its ramparts encircling granite-built, tightly-
packed houses, looks much the same now as it would have done in the
17th century, when the place was occupied by corsairs. The ferry glides
past Grand Jardin lighthouse, towards the ferry terminal. The channel
here is narrow, with Ile de Cézembre on one side and Ile Harbour on the
other; to the East are the extensive beaches off the holiday resort of
Paramé; to the West is Pointe de Dinard, covered in trees and flanked by
more beaches overlooked by expensive hotels and villas.

Owners of boats based on St Malo can hardly complain about a lack
of places to visit, all within a 30-mile radius. To the North are the Iles de
Chausey and Jersey; to the West is St Quay-Portrieux and the start of the
famous *Côte de Granit Rose*; to the East is Granville; and finally to the
South is Dinan, and the start of the waterways linking Brittany's North
coast with the North Biscay harbours of the West coast. Add to this the
delights of the town itself, and some boat owners will look no further for
their base across the Channel.

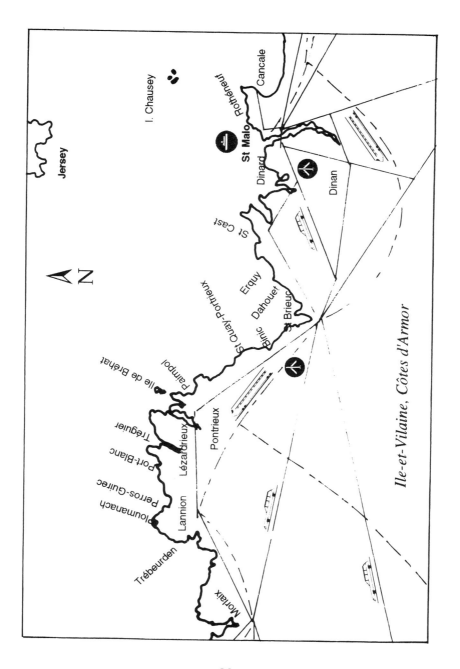

Ile-et-Vilaine, Côtes d'Armor

St Malo is steeped in history. It was from here in the 17th century that the famous corsairs sailed, with permission from the King of France to plunder English shipping. They seem to have been highly successful with their pirating. Their captains, treated as national heroes, accumulated vast wealth for the crown and for themselves.

It was around this period that the town, originally built on a small island of granite, was made virtually impenetrable. The forts, castle and gun emplacements on the ramparts, kept all raiders at bay and gave the place a certain independence.

Three centuries later, almost all the old buildings inside the walls were left in ruins. The Germans had occupied the fortifications, and the old town was to become a strategic target for the Allies. Although much of the town was destroyed, the ramparts, as we see them today, remained standing. After the war, the French were determined painstakingly to restore each building inside the wall as a faithful reproduction of what had been before. It is recognised as being one of the finest examples of post-war reconstruction.

Today, within the ramparts, is a lively town where the cobbled streets always seem to be packed with people. Amongst the souvenir shops are four-star restaurants, bistros, crêperies and bars, many of which open at about eight o'clock in the morning and close in the early hours. Those who want to build up an appetite or a thirst can climb the stone stairs to the top of the ramparts for a one-hour stroll, with ever changing views. Below, on one side, people may be dining in the open outside one of the restaurants; on the other side, the view may be of the long stretches of sand with Fort National in the distance.

A mere hundred metres from the old town is the giant Bassin Vauban. Many years ago, a visiting yacht here would pick up a mooring, lying stern on to the quay, with each yacht being provided with an individual gang plank. What a different picture to-day, with literally hundreds of yachts rafted up several deep against the pontoons. And yet the crews of almost every visiting yacht must agree that the charms of the place still remain.

St Malo is the only major port on Brittany's North coast. The entrance is straight forward, although there can be something of a strong cross-tide to contend with. Entering the Bassin Vauban, however, may be a new experience to some. There are two or three openings of the lock gates over a five hour period (two hours before HW and 3 hours after-sometimes extended for yachts at weekends during the season). At any time over this period, there might be a long wait because a large merchantman is entering or coming out.

Yachts waiting to enter the basin will collect outside, looking out for the 'stand-by' signal. Immediately the single green light comes on, the yachts outside start moving en masse towards the lock. Once inside, everyone hangs on to each other, as the water drops or rises. Depending on the time of day, on reaching the far end of the Bassin Vauban, a visiting yacht will be directed towards a space. This might be a berth conveniently close for getting ashore, but reached only by sliding the boat between many others, with only a few inches to spare on either side. When leaving, it may be necessary to walk the boat to clear water, and then wait for the departure 'stand-by' signal.

St Malo

35

This congestion in Bassin Vauban does not detract from the pleasure of having a berth here. With restricted times for entry and exit, the mooring charges are less than the neighbouring marina at St Servan, where a yacht can arrive and leave at any time except around low water. St Malo's Bassin Vauban is totally sheltered unlike St Servan's Port de Bas Sablon, where a strong North-Westerly can cause havoc on the pontoons.

During the season, larger craft locking into the Bassin Vauban, may be directed to lie alongside the Quaie St Louis (to port on entering). This is certainly picturesque, but much more in the public eye compared with a berth on the pontoons. Another possibility is for large craft to proceed up to the top of the harbour, pass through the lifting bridge, and berth at the West end of the Bassin Duguay-Trouin (named after one of St Malo's most distinguished corsairs).

St Malo has a hospitable yacht club (Societé Nautique de la Baie de St Malo). This is a useful *post-restante* address, avoiding the queues at the town post office. The one facility that is lacking in the Bassin Vauban is alongside fuelling. The nearest places for topping up the fuel tanks are St Servan (marina) or, on the West side of the Rance estuary, at Dinard's municipal marina. Neither of these fuelling jetties are available around low water. The St Malo alternative is a long walk with Jerry cans to the nearest garage, which is in the direction of the railway station.

St Malo is also a great place for children. There is a good beach just across the road from the pontoons. There are any amount of bus tours, starting from the nearby bus station. The Syndicate de Initiative (tourist office) overlooks the boats, along with the kiosks of several travel agents who can book bus and boat excursions or air passages. Very popular is a trip to Mont St Michel, and there are many boat trips either up the Rance to Dinan or out to sea to the Iles de Chausey. Within a few minutes walk from the boats, is the Castle, a museum and an aquarium (built into the walls of the ramparts). You can stroll along the causeway to the Fort National with the added excitement of getting back to the mainland before the tide gets too high (and remember that it is around these parts that the sea comes in with the speed of galloping horses!).

St Servan

The Rance estuary is an important yachting centre, with St Malo, neighbouring St Servan and sophisticated Dinard. The Port de Bas Sablons (St Servan) is a marina with all the usual facilities. Entry is possible except around low water (an illuminated panel on the North side shows the depth of water over the sill). Although it is more expensive, and open to North-Westerlies, some will prefer the convenience of being in the marina, particularly for a short stay. St Servan is much more than a suburb of St Malo, being a small town in its own right which was actually established before St Malo. It is a short walk from the marina to the shops and restaurants near the waterfront. The place is dominated by the 14th-century Tour Solidor, which was built on foundations dating back to the Roman occupation.

It takes a good half-hour to walk across the locks from St Servan to St Malo, and a brisk twenty minutes to reach the Brittany Ferry terminal via the beach at the head of the marina where there is a tidal swimming pool. If meeting someone off the ferry, it takes less time to row across from St Servan in the dinghy.

Dinard

On the other side of the Rance is the holiday resort of Dinard. There are many moorings some way off, but there is no escaping the tide here. With sufficient water, a visiting yacht may find a space in the small municipal yacht harbour which is reached up a dredged channel. The exclusive yacht club here organises many international sailing events. Dinard also has an International Horse Show, Tennis Tournaments, and one of the finest Casinos in France.

La Rance and Dinan

Leaving St Malo, St Servan or Dinard to proceed up river to the lovely old town of Dinan, it is necessary to know something about the water levels beyond the vast hydro-electric barrage, which generates power for a large area of France. This is well covered in the Cruising Guides. Suffice to say that the water level upstream of the barrage is artificially maintained at a minimum of chart datum plus 4m for around an 8 hour period during the day (mostly between 0700 and 2100). For about 4 hours during this period, the level is maintained at 8.5m. You can pick up the timetable for the workings of the Usine Maremotrice from any of the Rance yacht harbours or by listening to the recorded telephone message on 46.14.46. It also published daily in Ouest-France.

Within the 4 hour period (chart datum + 8.5m), there is plenty of water for sailing in lovely surroundings in the stretch of river between the barrage and St Suliac, which is the limit for an extended stay. Even here, the effects of opening up the sluices to generate the turbines will be felt.

Electricité de France warn boat owners that during the no-go hours, the water level can drop a whole metre in ten minutes!

Larger boats (with draught up to 1.6m) can make their way to Dinan with no restrictions on height. The best time to start this passage is three hours before high water. There is rarely a delay at the barrage lock (opening on the hour) so the passage can be planned to arrive off Mordreux with plenty of water to continue upriver to the next lock at Châtelier. This is worked over the 4 hour period when the artificial water level is being maintained at 8.5m. Outside this period, the narrow marked channel from St Suliac to the Châtelier lock quickly drains away to vast areas of mud. Once through Châtelier, where English boats always get a cheerful welcome from the lock keeper, there are no more worries about tide as this is the start of the Ille-et-Rance Canal, which continues right into the heart of Brittany, terminating at Rennes.

Dinan

You know you have arrived at Dinan when the giant viaduct comes into view. There is another very low Gothic bridge before the viaduct, which is the limit for any craft with more than 2.5m height above the water or drawing more than 1.2m. Below this first bridge, there is a long string of pontoon berths off the town quay. The crews of yachts berthed here have exclusive use of the smart shower block, with access through the harbour master's office. Conveniently close to the boats is a chandler, a crane (can be used for dismasting if continuing up the canal), fuel pumps, and a handful of shops and restaurants.

Dinan's town centre is through the impressive gateway (Porte du Jerzual); then there is a long climb up the narrow cobbled street between the old houses which lean inwards so far that their overhanging attics almost seem to touch. Several of these 15th and 16th-century houses are used as craft workshops, with their products displayed (and priced) in the window. Another way of reaching the town centre, is to climb the ramparts towards the castle, taking in a fine view of the town quay and the canal below.

Brittany waterways (The Vilaine River)

39

The author is a great enthusiast for the Brittany waterways. For someone whose boat is based at St Malo, these can provide a delightful alternative to slogging round the outside of Brittany to reach the yachting centres on the West coast. This waterway route right across Brittany can be achieved in 5 days, but it will be difficult to resist the temptation to dawdle through the Brittany countryside, and make it at least a week. Providing a yacht's height can be reduced to 2.5m (dropping the mast at Dinan or, more conveniently, at St Malo), then draught will be the all-important restriction. This is normally 1.2m, but in recent years because of the shortage of water, the authorities were having to issue a revised maximum draught. At one time this figure went as low as 0.9m. In the drought of 1992 the Ille-et-Rance canal was open only at weekends and restricted to craft passing through the locks in groups. Early in the season, when the traffic is light, the water level can usually be maintained by the lock keepers at 1.2m. A chapter is devoted to the Brittany waterways in the author's *'Brittany & Channel Islands Cruising Guide'*.

If leaving St Malo for a two or three week cruise or even a long weekend, the choice of places to visit is remarkable. Jersey and the Chausey Islands to the North together with Granville to the East, are briefly described in the Manche chapter. There are also two more places to the East worth a mention; these are Rothéneuf and Cancale (4 and 12 miles from St Malo).

Rothéneuf and Concale

These are two essentially day-time anchorages. Rothéneuf is a small holiday resort with a large natural drying harbour (ideal for twin-keelers). The entrance is very narrow, and needs someone on the foredeck to check the skipper's course through the offlying rocks. Rothéneuf is famous for the huge carvings in the rocks depicting faces and animals. Cancale is another holiday resort, with a drying harbour, and with drying sands extending a mile offshore (it is just in the Baie du Mont Saint Michel). The place is again ideal for twin-keelers, although sometimes a visiting yacht will find a place alongside one of the quays used by the fishing boats. Cancale is famous for its oysters.

Heading up to the West from St Malo, takes a yacht to by far and away the best cruising ground on the North coast. This is the 40-mile stretch of coastline between Paimpol and Trébeurden, known as the *Côte de*

Granit Rose. This is the most Northerly part of Brittany, with several marinas and excellent anchorages in amongst the pink, towering rock formations.

Navigation around this part of the coast might be challenging to some, particularly having to allow for a 4-knot tide (at springs). Providing the visibility is good, and the skipper is not trying to push the boat hard into wind against tide conditions, passage-making in the well-marked channels surrounded by the *Granit Rose* can be an exhilarating experience.

Even with a fair wind, smaller yachts setting out from the Rance in good time to catch the first of the West-going tide, may just fail to make the *Côte de Granit Rose*. It is 50 miles from the Rance estuary to the Trieux River. Assuming the best conditions, with the yacht making 5 knots through the water plus 6 hours of favourable tide (averaging, say, 2 knots at springs), then the distance covered over the 6 hour period would be 42 miles which would put the yacht off the Trieux estuary just in time to take the first of the flood up to Lézardrieux.

The boat owner will be fortunate to have the ideal conditions indicated above, and would be wise to take an early decision to put into one of the several anchorages or yacht basins en route between St Malo and the *Côte de Granit Rose*. In previous years, the choice of a secure berth in a yacht basin along this stretch of the coast was strictly limited. There is the commercial harbour of St Brieuc (le Légué), but this is a long deviation into the Baie de Saint Brieuc. To a lesser extent, this is also true of Binic, with the added risk of not studying the tide-tables closely, and being unable to enter or leave the yacht basin on exceptional neaps.

The string of holiday resorts, all packed into the 6-mile stretch of coastline to the West of the Rance estuary, are suitable for twin-keeled craft that can take the ground comfortably. St Lunaire, St Briac, Lancieux and St Jacut all have long, wide beaches (St Briac claims five, St Jacut eleven!). They are well protected from South-Westerlies, and in settled weather yachts can anchor off the resorts. A word of warning to those owners of twin-keeled craft who may not be familiar with the huge local range of tide – do not get neaped.

The next lot of possible stopping off places have either deep-water anchorages or wet basins behind lock gates. They are St. Cast where there is a marina development, Erquy, Port Dahouet, St Brieuc, Binic and St Quay-Portrieux.

St Cast

The St Cast anchorage is to the South of the Pointe de la Garde. This is something of a sailing centre, with many deep-water moorings; being only 10 miles from St. Malo, this can be a useful anchorage (except in North-Easterlies) if a yacht just fails to make St Malo on the tide. Apart from the Yacht Club de St Cast, which has a landing slip, there are no facilities ashore in this exclusive suburb of St Cast. It is a walk of about 1½ miles to the shops in St Cast proper, which is a holiday resort with a good beach. There are some visitors' buoys off the drying harbour used by fishing boats, and modest facilities ashore.

Erquy

Erquy, just in the Baie de Saint Brieuc, is a small, but busy, fishing port where the fishing boats monopolise the drying harbour and town quay. Yachts can anchor off the outside mole, but it is open to the South-West. There are many drying moorings (chains) either side of the old harbour wall. Erquy is a holiday resort with a fine beach. A popular restaurant overlooks the harbour, and it is a ten-minute walk round to the shops in the town.

Port Dahouet

Port Dahouet, 24 miles along the coast from St. Malo's Grand Jardin lighthouse, is reached through a tiny gap in the cliffs. Prior to the development of a marina here, Dahouet was not much visited by yachts, which shared the drying lines of moorings with the fishing boats. These drying moorings are still used by local boats, but a visiting yacht will cross the sill for a sheltered berth in the marina. There is sufficient water to enter Dahouet 3 hours either side of high water. For the high life, it is only a mile to the large holiday resort of Val André with its promenade and long, almost white beach, at the end of which is the drying Le Piegu harbour, where there are many sailing dinghies.

St Brieuc

St Brieuc, at the head of its own wide bay, is the capital town of the Côtes-d'Armor. There are train services to several of the cross-channel ports (St Malo via Dol; Caen via Dol; Cherbourg via Dol and Lison; Morlaix (Roscoff) direct. The harbour (Le Légué), is at the end of a gorge, with the town high up above on both sides, and linked by impressive viaducts. The harbour can only be approached with sufficient water over the sandbanks off the entrance. Yachts who do make this considerable detour into the Baie, use the inner of the two basins.

Binic

Still in the Baie de Saint Brieuc, but on the West side, is the yacht basin at Binic. Again, this is not greatly frequented by yachts on passage to or from the *Côte de Granit Rose*, and, with the development of St-Quay-Portrieux's deep harbour, Binic can seem an unnecessary diversion. The basin at Binic, now used exclusively by yachts, can be entered one hour either side of high water at springs (but for a shorter time towards neaps, and not at all when the tidal coefficient falls below 9.5m). The facilities for yachts here are good, and there is a bathing beach either side of the entrance.

St-Quay-Portrieux

The most Westerly of the Baie de Saint Brieuc's harbours is Portrieux. Before the major marina development here, this was a drying harbour used by a few fishing boats and a good number of local yachts, mostly using legs. Linked to neighbouring St Quay, the *commune* is an attractive holiday resort with several beaches. The Port de Plaisance is an extension into the deep-water built off the old harbour wall. There are pontoon berths for over 900 yachts, of which 10% are always reserved for visitors. A new quayside has been built for the fishing boats, which now have deep-water moorings inside the outer mole.

Côte de Granit Rose

Once out of the Baie de Saint Brieuc, a yacht is entering the waters off the *Côte de Granit Rose*. The chart highlights the rugged coastline, with its many offlying dangers; it cannot, however, give an impression of the grandeur of the coastline, with its huge pink-coloured rocks, weirdly shaped over the years by the elements. This is obviously a coastline to be treated with some respect. The tide runs at about 4 knots off the coast, and wind against tide can cause steep, short seas, particularly off the Ile de Bréhat, where the offlying dangers extend for 6 or 7 miles. The last thing the author wants to do is put people off visiting this wild coastline. The French buoyage system here is of a reassuringly high standard, with many large, conspicuous beacon towers used to great effect.

Paimpol

The first of the ports on this stretch of coastline is Paimpol, at the head of a large drying bay. Towards low water, the bay is transformed into a huge expanse of mud. There are well marked channels through the shallows to the outer jetties of the port. The lock is worked HW -2/+1 at springs, but over a lesser period at neaps (and may not operate at all on exceptionally neap tides). The old basin is still used by commercial craft; most of the No. 2 basin, has been taken over by yachts on pontoons. The Cruising branch of the Centre Nautique des Glénans is located here. Paimpol plays host to an annual gathering of traditional boats, which is becoming an important event on the French gaffers' calendar. The port is conveniently near to the centre of the town.

Ile de Bréhat

For years, the Ile de Bréhat has been a firm favourite of the author; this is in spite of drying out alongside the stone jetty at the top of Port Clos, and very nearly getting neaped. These days, it is not so easy to use the jetty, because around high water the *vedettes* from Pointe de l'Arcouest seem to arrive every few minutes, berthing alongside the jetty with boatloads of holiday makers. In those days we did not have legs for the boat, and Bréhat is the sort of place where the twin-keelers or boats with legs are at a considerable advantage over fin keeled craft.

The Ile de Bréhat is in the estuary of the Trieux river. If the tide dictates it, the approach is easier entering the river proper, passing to the West of Bréhat and then doubling back down Le Ferlas channel to approach Port Clos and La Chambre anchorage from the South. Bréhat, just three-quarters of a mile long and 2 miles wide, is the largest of the numerous pink islands and rocks that make up this archipelago in the estuary of the Trieux river. Bréhat is actually two islands, linked by an isthmus. The North of Bréhat has a spectacularly rocky shore, with Bréhat's easily identifiable pink granite lighthouse on the Northern extremity of the island. At the neck of the isthmus, on the West side, is the anchorage of La Corderie, which is bleak and wild, but may be preferable to La Chambre at the South end of the island, if there are strong South-Westerlies.

There is virtually nothing on this North end of the island except for the wild scenery. The South island is more welcoming, with plenty of shops and restaurants in Le Bourg and many marvellous views from the pine woods up above Port Clos. There is a crisscross of paths on the South island with some delightful walks.

The main anchorage at the Southern end of the island is La Chambre. The problem here is that at the height of the season it gets very crowded, and a shift of the wind can make the anchorage uncomfortable. There is a strategically placed wash-barrier to protect the anchorage from some of the swell, but it can be difficult for deep keeled craft to anchor out of the tide. Owners of twin-keeled craft can be very smug, for they can simply drive the boat up to the top end of the anchorage, to rest on the firm sands. This, too, is more convenient for the shops and bars in Le Bourg. Twin-keeled craft can also dry out in Port Clos, providing they are well clear of the three slipways used by the *vedettes* according to the tide. There is a good beach between La Chambre and Port Clos.

Ile de Bréhat

Lézardrieux

Ten miles up the Trieux River is Lézardrieux, which for many years has been the most popular port for English yachts visiting the North coast of Brittany. There is a marina here, with many visitors' moorings in the river. Ashore is a pleasant yacht club where, most of the time, the English outnumber the French. The village is a climb of about ½ a mile from the marina. Below Lézardrieux are many sheltered anchorages in most attractive surroundings.

Pontrieux

Just up-river of the Lézardrieux marina is a suspension bridge (17m clearance at high water springs). Beyond the bridge are a couple of beacon towers, after which there are no marks to indicate the deep water channel to cross a vast expanse of water (towards high water). This should not deter boat owners from visiting Pontrieux – a gem of a place a further 7 miles upriver. At mid tide, the navigator might be concerned that much of the water has been replaced by vast expanses of mud. At high water neaps, there is fact a minimum of 3 metres of water all the way up to the Pontrieux lock. A yacht drawing 1.4 metres can leave Lézardrieux about 2½ hours before high water. The yacht will remain in the deep water if the starboard-hand beacon tower (Begantymeur) is lined up with a point on the bridge astern, roughly a third of the way along from the East bank. Using this back transit, the yacht will be heading towards isolated white buildings, after which the river narrows.

The winding Trieux then passes through a gorge and then wooded countryside. There are no signs of civilisation until, round a sharp bend, the magnificent 15th century Château de la Roche-Jagu, topped with many ornamental chimneys, comes into view. In the river below, are pools in which a yacht can anchor in minimum 3m of water. The lock at Pontrieux is worked for 2 hours before and an hour after high water. Visiting yachts line the quayside and receive a friendly welcome from the harbour master or his assistant. The facilities are good, and the town (about 20 minutes walk from the Port) is charming. Pontrieux is well-off the beaten tourist track, so do not expect any night-life here.

Pontrieux

Tréguier

The Tréguier River is approximately 5 miles West of the Trieux River, but it is many more miles to sail round. It can be more difficult to enter the Tréguier river, with its rock-strewn entrance and offlying dangers extending beyond the Heaux lighthouse. There are some transits to home in on, but they can be quite difficult to identify, particularly if viewed against the sun. There are two channels into the river – the Grande Passe to the West of les Heaux and the Passe de la Gaine which is narrow, passing close to the East side of les Heaux. There is only 1.2m of water in the Passe de la Gaine at MLWS, so a yacht cannot afford to wander. The river is scenically as attractive as its neighbour. 6 miles upriver is the marina and many visitors' buoys off the town quay. One word of caution, the tide fairly rips through the pontoons, and at certain times great care is needed to manoeuvre. Tréguier is a small town, with its own cathedral, a town square and a good selection of restaurants and cafés. Like Lézardrieux, a bridge (11m) spans the river just above the marina; the upper reaches, navigable by small craft for another 3 miles, are used only by small fishing boats which lie off la Roche Derrien, where the channel dries 5.1m.

Port Blanc

6 miles to the West of the Tréguier River is the small, natural harbour of Port Blanc. Some boats from the West of England prefer to set off to their home port from here because it is the shortest crossing, and they can leave at any time. The entrance is difficult to locate, as one gap in the rocks looks very much like another. There is a lighthouse, but it is small (17m) and can be obscured by trees. On both sides of the anchorage are towering rock formations which the author remembers all too vividly, having got caught inside when the wind strengthened from the North-West. The penalty was a miserable 24 hours spent waiting until the gap in the rocks could be negotiated to reach the safety of the sea outside. A few fishing boats are based here in what is reckoned to be the wildest scenery on Brittany's North coast. Port Blanc has a restaurant and a few shops.

Perros-Guirec

Perros is another of those places on the North coast where the fishing boats have gradually been pushed out by pleasure craft. The port is at the end of the large drying Anse de Perros, and at low water is about 2 miles from the sea. The old drying fishing harbour was little more than a jetty, against which both fishing boats and yachts on passage dried out. Ashore, Perros was no more than a village with a Restaurant du Port and a bar or two. The place was transformed by building a lock half way along the jetty and then a retaining wall right the way across the entrance to the old port. A few fishing boats still dry out along the jetty, but inside the retaining wall accommodation for 600 yachts has been provided. Now, overlooking the harbour, are great blocks of flats, with restaurants, snack bars, souvenir shops and much more besides (including a yacht chandler). Whilst one might regret the passing of the ambience of the old port, the marina facilities are excellent. The single gate opens for around 2½ hours at springs and 1 hour at neaps.

The fashionable nearby resort together with the port make up the commune of Perros-Guirec. It is about half a mile from the port by main road into the town centre. The alternative is a delightful walk along the Boulevard de la Mer and then by path past the resort's fashionable beaches at Tréstrignel and Tréstraou. If the walk is continued along the clifftop path, this eventually leads to Ploumanach.

Ploumanach

Ploumanach

Of all the marvellous scenery along the *Côte de Granit Rose*, the entrance to Ploumanach must be the most impressive. A pink Château (Château Costaères) overlooks the entrance and anyone who has been here in a boat must put it at the top of the list of most favoured places along Brittany's North coast. Until recent years, it was seen on a large scale chart as a small drying harbour, with rocks seemingly everywhere in the approach. Most yachts visiting the place then, would simply poke their noses in towards high water, anchoring for an hour or two off the Château.

With the construction of a sill across the narrow entrance to the drying harbour and then the provision of moorings, Ploumanach has appeared on the itineraries of more and more yachts cruising the North Brittany coast. The harbour can be entered 3½ hours either side of high water, when there will be at least 1.5m over the sill. Navigating has been greatly simplified both from the East and the West, picking up the no.1 starboard hand pole beacon and then following the subsequent poles marking the channel. Most of the moorings have 1.5m water. Tidal gauges mark the level of water over the sill at beacons 6 and 12. The harbour is totally protected, but you do need a dinghy to get ashore where there is a shower block. Ploumanach has several restaurants, plenty of shops and a good bathing beach (to port on entering).

Les Sept Isles

Two miles North of Ploumanach are Les Sept Iles, which consist of two main islands – Ile aux Moines and Ile de Bono – and many more islets and rocks. There is a landing slip on Ile aux Moines, mostly used these days for dropping off visitors from the *vedettes* that sail here from the beach at Perros-Guirec. Landing on Ile Bono is prohibited because it is a bird sanctuary. There is an anchorage, protected from the North, off Ile aux Moines' landing slip. The time to visit Les Sept Iles is during the puffin breeding season, when they can be seen in great numbers (from a safe distance).

Trébeurden

The most westerly yacht harbour along the *Côte de Granit Rose*, and still in the Côtes d'Armor, is Trébeurden. Until recently, there was an anchorage here in the lee of Ile Milliau. Now the place has been partially transformed with a major development plan. This transformation is qualified because in 1991, the developers lost a battle against the local environmentalists who were not objecting to the new marina, but to the flats and shops planned around the new port. The developers were ordered to stop work, by which time the yacht harbour had almost been completed. It is planned to open in 1992; no doubt the yachting magazines will keep us informed.

Lannion

The last port in the Côtes d'Armor is Lannion, which is 4 miles up the Léguer river. The river is particularly attractive, and by careful use of the depthsounder, a visiting yacht may find a deep-water pool in which to anchor in delightful surroundings. These pools, either side of the small village of le Yaudet, are created by the constant dredging for sand. Apart from this deep-water, the whole of the Léguer dries. Lannion is a good shopping centre, with many fine examples of 15th and 16th Century buildings. The commercial port is a useful place to visit for a couple of hours around high water.

> ### Finistère
> Morlaix – Roscoff – l'Abervrac'h – Ouessant (Ushant) – Brest – Port
> Launay – Châteaulin – Camaret – Morgat – Douarnenez – Audierne –
> Loctudy – Benodet – Iles de Glénan – Port-la-Forét – Concarneau –
> Port Manech

Cross-channel port: Roscoff
(see also Travel Section)

The most westerly of the Channel yacht bases is in the Rade de Brest. Although not so conveniently placed in relation to the Channel ferry terminals, a permanent berth here does offer any number of cruising possibilities.

The Moulin Blanc yacht harbour, in the Rade de Brest, is an ideal springboard for yachts (even of a modest size) to cruise Southwards along the West coast of Brittany, which some consider the finest cruising ground in France.

Starting out from the UK, an attempted cruise to and from North Biscay, can be something of a gamble, particularly for smaller craft. With unsettled weather, the skipper may decide it is prudent to shorten the passages, and opt for a much-sailed (but time consuming) itinerary. From, say, the Solent, a yacht will make for Guernsey, and then cross to the Trieux estuary on the North Brittany coast, and from there make short passages with the tide, stopping off in the Morlaix estuary, and then at l'Abervrac'h, Morgat and Audierne.

Longer passages from the UK may still mean negotiating the Four Channel between the French mainland and Ushant, and then rounding the infamous Pointe du Raz. This formidable landmark, off which the tide can pour through the Raz de Sein at 6 knots, cannot be attempted with the tide against a strong wind (the author has had to wait 7 days at Douarnenez for the right conditions to round the Raz, reaching the North Biscay harbours with only a day or two's cruising left before handing the boat over to another member of the family).

After the Pointe du Raz, the next landmark along the coast is the Pointe de Penmarch; beyond which the sea is reputed to turn to a deeper shade of blue and the weather becomes noticeably warmer. Palm trees and mimosa flourish here in the mild climate, giving some of the harbours an almost Mediterranean flavour. The yacht will then be in North Biscay where the choice of ports, marinas and anchorages is so

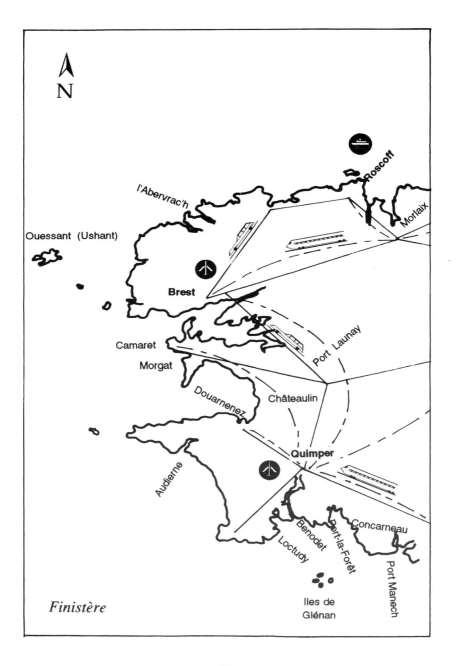

extensive that the pilot books of the area run to almost 300 pages. And the distance from the Rade de Brest to Penmarch is less than 40 miles!

Even with a month's holiday, it may be too much like hard work to reach the North Biscay harbours from the UK and still have time to explore and then sail the boat back. Belle Ile may have to wait for another year, when the island can be reached without a long slog into South-Westerlies. And how much more relaxing to cruise these parts without having to keep one eye on the barometer and the other on the calendar.

Roscoff and Baie de Morlaix

The Brittany Ferries terminal at Roscoff, on Finistere's North coast, is just inside the Baie de Morlaix which is a large expanse of water with several well-known anchorages used by yachts on passage. Approaching the Baie from the sea, the dangers in the rock-strewn entrance are well-marked with beacon towers and the imposing Château du Taureau. Two rivers run into the Baie – the Morlaix and the Penzé.

Geographically, the bay is between the Roscoff ferry terminal to the West and Primel to the East. There is a deep-water anchorage at Primel, off the breakwater used by the Le Diben fishing fleet. Seven miles further East of the Pointe de Primel (and still claimed by the local tourist office as being part of the Baie de Morlaix) is Locquirec – a drying harbour and popular holiday resort in the estuary of the River Douron, which is the Départemental boundary between Finistère and the Côte d'Armor.

Although much of the actual Baie dries around low water, this is something of a sailing centre. There is always water in the lower reaches of the Morlaix and Penzé Rivers, where there are many moorings. At high water it is possible to take the Morlaix river right up to the old town, and lock into the wet basin. There is a waiting list for permanent berths here, but a visiting yacht can stay for a week or two, and it is a convenient place for changing crews. The Penzé River is a great contrast to the Morlaix, with little else apart from the moorings, tranquillity and great expanses of mud. Between these river estuaries is a very different anchorage, off the popular holiday resort of Carantec which claims to have seven beaches.

Roscoff is the one cross-channel port where it would be difficult to leave the boat unattended for any length of time. Brittany Ferries have their own terminal at Port Bloscon, which is South-East of Roscoff's drying harbour. Although there are a few moorings off Port Bloscon, these should be considered for emergency use only in bad weather. Roscoff itself, consists of an outer harbour (Port Neuf) which is mostly used by small coasters, fishing boats and, around high water, the Ile de Batz ferries. The only place where a visiting fin-keel yacht can dry out is in the inner harbour (Vieux Port), but advice should be sought before using the jetty as the bottom may be foul. To the West of the Ar Chaden light tower are some deep-water mooring buoys, protected from the South-West. These provide little more than somewhere to stop to await the turn of the tide, and are too far out to row to the shore.

The Chenal de l'Ile de Batz is the well-marked deep-water channel between Roscoff and the Ile de Batz. Taking this inshore passage is safe, although the tide runs strongly (5 knots at springs), so the crews of most yachts will see little of Roscoff and Batz as they hurtle by. Ile de Batz is two miles long and a mile wide, and has a sheltered drying harbour (Porz Kernoch) which is ideal for twin-keeled craft. By using long jetties extending out to the deep-water, the *vedettes* taking holiday-makers to and from Batz can run at any state of the tide. The island caters for these visitors with a restaurant, a crêperie, bars and shops.

Ile de Batz

l'Abervrac'h

Between Roscoff and l'Abervrac'h (the next popular anchorage to the West) is 30 miles of the bleakest coastline along the whole of the French side of the Channel. Sometimes referred to as the *Côte des Naufrageurs*, the dangers extend up to three miles offshore. The entrance to l'Abervrac'h looks intimidating on the chart and would normally be given a miss in poor visibility. A few years ago, the local lifeboat foundered on the rocks in the entrance with appalling loss of life in an accident that has never really been explained. Night entry is perhaps easier than going in by day, with the powerful light on Ile Vierge and well lit transits that take a boat right up to the marina.

l'Abervrac'h is another of those ports used mainly by yachts on passage. There is a yacht club here, a small marina and many visitors' buoys. The place itself is only a village where you can buy bread and croissant at the local *tabac*; the shops are reached by climbing up the steep road for 2 miles to Lannilis. The attractive upper reaches of the river are navigable with sufficient water for a further 2 miles as far as Paluden. If care is taken to anchor in the right spot off Paluden's drying quays, a visiting boat (1.2m draught) can remain afloat at low water. Ashore there are a few houses, a bistro and a hotel.

The next 30 miles, heading first to the West and then turning the corner of Brittany to sail South, is in parts as bleak as the neighbouring stretch of coastline to the East of l'Abervrac'h. From a navigational point of view, sailing round to the West side of Finistère is much more interesting. There are two more Abers (Rivers) – l'Aberbenoît and l'Aber Ildut. Both have anchorages but they are not much used by visiting yachts who will mostly be pressing on, taking the full six hours of tide reach Brest, Camaret or Morgat.

There may be the opportunity for the navigator to take a short cut from l'Abervrac'h to the Four Channel by going inside the Roches de Portsall. There are very few conventional navigation marks, and it is mostly a matter of lining up rocks in transit (providing, of course, these have been correctly identified). Some would say it is only suitable for boat owners who have local knowledge. Just to add some encouragement to the enthusiast, taking this inshore short-cut leaves the wreck of the Amoco Cadiz to seaward. This is the most notorious wreck around this coastline in recent years. As she broke up, the tanker's cargo of oil did immeasurable damage to sea-life and polluted the beaches of the few local holiday resorts.

The Chenal du Four is the 12 mile stretch of water with the Four lighthouse at one end and the Pointe St Mathieu at the other. The Ile de Molène and Ushant to seaward give some protection. The tide is strong (5 knots at springs), and small craft should avoid wind against tide conditions or attempting the Four in poor visibility.

Rade de Brest and Moulin Blanc

The Rade de Brest is an expanse of 40 square miles of almost landlocked water, reached through the Goulet de Brest. This is the tide-ripped, mile-wide narrows between the Brest shore line and the Presque'île de Quelern. Wind against tide (4.6 knots at springs) produces some short, uncomfortable seas, but apart from this qualification, the Rade can be safely entered day or night as one would expect with a large part of the French Navy based here.

With the boat already at Brest, the skipper can take the first opportunity to round the Pointe du Raz which is only 18 miles from the Rade entrance and less from nearby Morgat. If the weather is particularly unsettled, there will still be plenty of opportunities for sailing locally. Surrounded by hills, and fed by six different rivers, the Rade de Brest and neighbouring Baie de Douarnenez provide a most attractive cruising ground where a boat owner could happily spend three weeks and always have some new place to visit.

There is only one place in the Rade de Brest where a yacht can find a permanent marina berth, and this is the Port de Plaisance du Moulin Blanc (although of late, one or two British yachts might be found based, at least for the summer months, several miles inland in the canalised section of the Aulne River).

Moulin Blanc is 8 miles inland from the Goulet de Brest. There are all the facilities one might expect at this major marina development (one of the largest in Brittany with 1,200 places). It is about three miles from the centre of Brest, in the bleak outskirts of the city. There is, however, a regular shuttle service of small buses between the Centre Ville and the marina. A restaurant, bar and pizzeria are on the marina site, with one or two local shops for basic provisions. The marina office is in a large building where the staff will provide much useful local information. There is a man-made beach nearby with various obstacles making up a children's assault course.

For those who want to limit their cruising to the Rade de Brest, this is well covered on the Admiralty chart 3427 (scale 1:30 000). Leaving the marina and heading North-East for a mile, will take a yacht under the suspension bridge Albert-Louppe (clearance 28m) spanning the Elorne river. This section is packed with deep-water moorings off Le Passage where the headquarters of the Yacht Club de la Rade de Brest is situated.

At half-tide, a yacht can continue upriver for a further six miles, between spasmodically marked mudbanks, to the old market town of Landerneau. There are a few visitors' drying moorings from which it can be something of a struggle to get ashore. There are no facilities for visiting yacht crews apart from a shower block at a nearby camp site.

To the South-West of the Moulin Blanc marina is Brest's Port de Commerce and the extensive military port (Rade Abri on the chart). Yachts are not normally permitted to use either of these ports.

The most attractive area for cruising within the Rade is undoubtedly the Aulne River. The wide Aulne estuary contains two bays – l'Auberlach and Daoulas, where boats can spend the night on deep-water moorings or continue up the Daoulas River at half-tide and dry out alongside the quay in the small commercial harbour of Tinduff. 3 miles beyond Logona-Daoulas is the start of the river proper. At Landévennec, the Aulne curves right round almost meeting itself and then curls sharply back again. Port Maria, which is Landévennec's harbour, consists of a line of ten deep-water moorings which are open to the North-West and where there is no escaping the tide. Ashore there is a slipway, a drying-out area and showers at the camp site. The fine example of a Benedictine Abbey attracts a large number of visitors to Landévennec.

The moorings marked on the chart North of the tiny, wooded Ile de Térénez are for a varied fleet of derelict ships. Some yacht crews choose to spend the night sharing the giant mooring buoys, but landing on the ships is positively forbidden, and there is nothing ashore here apart from extensive woodland.

There are one or two anchorages between the Ile de Térénez and the Pont de Térénez (clearance 27m) but it is difficult to get out of the strong tide. Chart 3427 finishes just beyond the bridge, but this should not deter boat owners from continuing further upriver at half-tide.

It is another 12 miles from the Térénez suspension bridge to the Guily-Glaz lock (worked two hours either side of HW). Given a reasonable rise of water, large craft occasionally make their way up the river and beyond the lock into the canal where there is 3m of water as far as Châteaulin.

The basic rule for navigating these uncharted waters is to keep to the outside of the bends (at mid-tide, extensive mud banks can be seen extending some distance from the inside bends). Keep to the middle when the river is straight. It is lovely countryside here, and for some deep-keeled craft this inland cruising may be something of a new, and pleasurable experience.

There are only two possible stopping places between Térénez Bridge and the Guily-Glaz lock – these are Trégarvan and Le Passage. Both have landing slips and moorings; Trégarvan also has a bar, a church and lovely views of the river. Elsewhere, either there will be insufficient water at low tide or the tidal stream will be uncomfortably strong.

A couple of miles before the lock, the river divides in two. Turn to starboard here (the other branch of the river is a dead-end, spanned by a motorway bridge).

Beyond the lock, the Aulne Maritime becomes the Nantes-a-Brest canal. There is a giant railway viaduct (clearance 41m), and then Port-Launay, which is a large village with plenty of room to moor alongside the tree-lined quays on the left bank. There is a conveniently situated boulangerie overlooking the quayside, and a few shops around the square. Port-Launay also has a waterside restaurant with its own landing stage.

A mile further on is Châteaulin with its town quays on both sides of the canal. The author has been here several times and no mooring fees have ever been requested. The place has been written up once or twice in the yachting magazines, but prior to this only a handful of British yachts knew of this delightful location. Not unreasonably, they were keeping Châteaulin a secret to themselves.

These days, the town tries in a modest way to encourage visiting yachts. A recreation centre, with showers, has been built on the right bank. For craft moored on this side of the river, about 5 minutes walk away is a huge hypermarket where the prices of provisions and fuel are amazingly competitive. They also have a cafeteria/restaurant on the premises, providing a three-course meal for astonishingly few francs.

For almost all craft, the navigable waterway stops at Châteaulin. The Nantes-à-Brest canal continues for another 85 kilometres and 43 self-operated locks to just beyond Port de Carhaix, where a hydro scheme permanently blocks the canal at Mur-de-Bretagne (Lac du Guerledan). This section of canal beyond Châteaulin is, however, restricted to craft with 1.10m draught and 2.50m headroom.

Port Launay

Leaving the Aulne River, and moving on to the South side of the Rade de Brest, one glance at chart 3427 is enough to discourage anyone from entering these waters. Nearly all of what look like useful anchorages are, on the chart, marked with purple pecked lines and labelled 'Entry prohibited', 'Anchoring prohibited' or 'Oyster Beds'. Most of the jetties and the harbour on Ile Longue are exclusively for use by the French Navy, and trespassers should beware.

There are one or two exceptions. On the East side of Pointe de Lanvéoc is a slipway and some moorings well protected from South-Westerlies. It is about 1.5 km to the village, and there is a nearby camp site with showers. There are more deep-water moorings close inshore off Le Fret which is a fishing village linked to Brest by a ferry service. There are showers available near the drying harbour.

Another possibility is to anchor off Roscanvel, on the East side of the Presqu'île de Quelern. Approaching this anchorage, yachts must keep well clear of the West side of Ile Longue. Like Le Fret, Roscanvel is a small drying harbour with an anchorage off the jetty well protected from South-Westerly weather. Quelern is a perfect example of a peninsula, which, at its narrowest, is only half-a-mile wide. The crews of yachts anchored off Roscanvel could land here, cross to the other side of the peninsula, and then walk on a couple of miles to Camaret.

Camaret

Camaret

By sea it is about 5 miles to Camaret from the East end of the Goulet de Brest. This one-time fishing port is much used by visiting yachts as a passage-harbour between the North coast of Brittany and the Biscay harbours on the West coast. The entrance to Camaret is very straightforward, by day or night, and the only problem here can be in North-Easterly winds, when the outside yacht harbour is exposed. The pontoons here can get very crowded with craft lying two or three deep.

Overlooking the yacht harbour is the distinctive Tour Dorée which was built by Vauban as a great fortress. In amongst the foundations is a shower block for the use of visiting crews. Off the end of the lifeboat slip are several visitors' moorings. Another possibility is Port Styvel at the end of a dredged channel leading towards the town's drying quay from which the pontoons extend. These pontoons are more sheltered, but mostly monopolised by local boats. The inner harbour is ideal for twin-keelers to dry out on firm sand.

A walk round from the pierhead to the town quay passes old hulls of *langoustiers* which serve as a reminder of the importance of Camaret, a good few years ago, as a thriving fishing port. They built these massive wooden boats on the beach, and sailed them as far afield as Morocco in search of the langoustine which is a bit like a large version of the Dublin Bay prawn and a great delicacy in Brittany.

Diesel is available at certain times from the pump by the lifeboat slip. There is a useful Co-operative Maritime here for basic chandlery at reasonable prices. Much of the town now caters for tourists with lively bars, restaurants and the inevitable souvenir shops. The beach here, to seaward of the sea wall, is grey sand and stones and not much used; anyone looking for a really fine beach in the vicinity will find one by taking the road and then the track leading to the Anse de Pen-Hat.

Morgat

Morgat is on the West side of the Baie de Douarnenez and a mere 8 km overland from Camaret. To reach Morgat by sea from the North, involves rounding four headlands and negotiating the inshore Chenal de Toulinguet. Once in the Baie de Douarnenez, a yacht can head up towards Morgat in clear waters (apart from the isolated rocks 2.5 miles to the South-East). Day or night entry to the marina is straightforward.

Many years ago, Morgat was a small drying fishing harbour, but like so many places on the Brittany coast, the local fishing fleet has almost disappeared to be replaced by an extensive marina development. The Port de Plaisance at Morgat is well protected against winds from any direction. There are alongside fuelling facilities in the old harbour and the usual shower block by the Port Office.

Morgat

Morgat is actually one half of the *commune* Crozon-Morgat which is an attractive holiday resort. The centre of Crozon-Morgat, with many shops and restaurants, is about a mile away from the marina. The beach here is excellent, and long enough to accommodate the many visitors on fine days during the holiday season. There are regular boat trips from the harbour to explore the nearby grottos. For anyone who likes walking, a path leads up to the woods above the marina, and from there you follow the arrows to the Pointe de Morgat for some magnificent views across the bay.

The Baie de Douarnenez is an area of about 60 square miles. Being so open, it can get choppy, but in settled conditions it is a great area for simply enjoying the sailing with nothing to worry about except the isolated rocks referred to above. The tidal streams here are weak. Apart from temporary, daytime anchorages around the bay, there is, of course, Douarnenez itself.

Douarnenez

This is one of the busiest fishing ports in Brittany, where yachts are positively discouraged from using the main harbour or the Port du Rosmeur. The quaysides here are exclusively for landing the catch which is mostly mackerel, tunny and sardine. Close to the quays are vast buildings which house the fish market and sardine canning factories.

Yachts can anchor off Port du Rosmeur in moderate shelter and with a long row to the shore. Visiting yachts are expected to use neighbouring Tréboul Marina, which is to the West of the main harbour, with an entrance channel West of Ile Tristan.

Tréboul is a small marina, but not all that many visiting yachts choose to make this detour right up to the far end of the Bay. Most will prefer, if the weather is set fair, to continue Southwards to the Biscay harbours; if the weather is unsettled, then they will usually make for Morgat or Camaret. They miss out on a friendly welcome at Tréboul, where the marina staff can nearly always accommodate visitors.

Continuing along the entrance channel, past the Tréboul marina on the right, there are drying berths at Port Rhu alongside the quays either side of the high roadbridge. Port Rhu has a highly recommended maritime museum which includes some remarkable exhibits on the water. It is a good half hour's walk from Tréboul into the centre of Douarnenez via the roadbridge – much quicker to row across to the Douarnenez side of the entrance channel and walk on from there.

Douarnenez

Any boat owner based in the Rade de Brest, who is looking for the thrills and spills of more exciting sailing, will find plenty of challenges around these parts to keep the adrenalin flowing. There is Ushant (or Ouessant as it is known in France) and neighbouring Ile Molène. Anyone contemplating a visit to these islands should be warned that there are stretches of water here which, under some conditions, must be avoided because of the exceptionally strong tides. A yacht has only to wander a little off course in the approaches to find herself in the Passage de Fromveur and in an 8-knot race. There is an alternative – take one of the boat trips from Brest or Le Conquet.

Mention has already been made of the Pointe du Raz and the Raz de Sein which are well covered in all the pilot books of the area. On the seaward side of the Raz de Sein is the Ile de Sein, surrounded by rocks which extend six miles out to the West; the tidal overfalls extend still further, to beyond the Chaussée de Sein buoy.

Ile de Sein

For most yacht crews, the small, flat Ile de Sein flashes by as the navigator shapes a course to shoot through the Raz as quickly as possible. The Ile de Sein is actually easier than suggested by the chart. There are conspicuous marks to go in on, and the tide does not rip through the approaches to the Ile de Sein as strongly as it does in the middle of the Raz. It came as something of a surprise to the author to learn from the owner of a French boat based at Morgat, that he frequently went out there, sailing into the Ile de Sein anchorage because his boat had no engine. The island's inhabitants mostly make a living from the sea, but in recent years they have adjusted to catering for tourists who, during the season, arrive in an Audierne-based *vedette*. It should perhaps be emphasised that slack water round here is for a short duration, and the Ile de Sein, Ushant and Molene should only be attempted by those with experience of navigating in strong tides in unfamiliar surroundings.

Audierne, Penmarch and Loctudy

Passage-making Southwards, apart from Audierne, there is nowhere to stop along the 20 miles of flat, featureless coastline between the Pointe du Raz and the Pointe de Penmarch. Audierne, being only 9 miles from the Raz de Sein, is a useful stopping off place; perhaps a few hours could be usefully spent here to get the tide right off the Pointe du Raz, when returning from the North Biscay harbours. The small town is on the drying River Goyen. There are a few buoys for visitors in the deep-water Ste. Evette anchorage, but it is a long walk into the town from here.

Considering its significance in cruising terms, the Pointe de Penmarch comes as something of an anti-climax. The land here is flat, with offlying dangers extending a mile offshore. These are marked by a lighthouse (Menhir) with Eckmuhl lighthouse at the end of the Pointe (towering over a smaller, disused one). After Penmarch, the first of the North Biscay sailing harbours and anchorages come up thick and fast. It is just 14 miles from the Pointe to the Anse de Benodet. On the West side of the bay is Loctudy, where the fishing boats share the anchorage with an increasing number of yachts. The small, dredged harbour is reserved exclusively for fishing boats which are something of a local tourist attraction, particularly when the catch is being landed on the quayside for the local fish market. There is a Port de Plaisance off the West side of the Port de Pêche.

Loctudy is on the South side of the narrow entrance to the Rivière Pont l'Abbé; on the North side is the fishing village of Ile Tudy which is actually a peninsula, providing shelter to the many moorings just above the river entrance. There are shops at both Loctudy and Ile Tudy which also has a fine beach. Pont-l'Abbé is 3 miles up the river. A yacht drawing 1.2m can sail up to the town 3 hours either side of high water.

The channel is well marked right up to the tree-lined quays of this ancient town.

Bénodet

Neighbouring Bénodet displays a certain exclusivity even before a yacht has arrived. The Yacht Club de Odet, with its green lawns and pine trees, is in a prominent position on the Pointe du Coq, overlooking the estuary of the Odet River. Beyond the Pointe, the river narrows with the town quays of Bénodet on one side and Sainte-Marine on the other. Standing on the quay at Bénodet, there are moorings upriver as far as the eye can see. The place is a Mecca for yachting and, with its small beach in the entrance, is also a sophisticated holiday resort.

There are two marinas here, both of which accommodate visiting yachts. Just beyond the town, on the starboard side when entering, is the Port de Penfoul which is the smaller of the two, and a boat-owner may well have to make do with one of the visitors' buoys instead of a pontoon berth. It can sometimes be difficult to manoeuvre into or leave a pontoon berth here because of the tide. There are alongside fuelling facilities, and a shower block. It is a walk of about 10 minutes to the shops in the town, and a little longer to the yacht club. The café/bar facing the port stays open until the early hours. The other marina, with over 70 berths for visitors, is Port de Sainte-Marine, across the river opposite Bénodet. Sainte-Marine is a large village; for anyone wanting the town, there is a convenient ferry between Sainte-Marine and Bénodet.

Many years ago, it was possible to navigate a boat right up the Odet River to the centre of Quimper. Nowadays, there is a fixed bridge a mile below the town. The river is very attractive, but if contemplating anchoring in these upper reaches, beware the flood which can reach 6 knots at springs. The strength of the flood is considerably less at the top end of the river where a yacht can stay at anchor for an hour or two. Old Quimper was the capital of the *Cournouaille Region*. Anyone interested in traditional Breton costume, dances and folk-music should be at Quimper for the annual Fêtes de Cournouaille. From Bénodet there is a bus service and also boat trips to Quimper.

Iles de Glénan

Anyone who wants to get away from the bustling sailing activity of Benodet, needs look no further than the Iles de Glénan, which are just 10 miles South-East of the Odet river. The Glénans form an archipelago of nine tiny islands, with many more offlying rocks and shoals. This was the first location of the now famous world-wide sailing school, founded in 1947 by ex-members of the French Resistance. Every week, in the season, boat-loads of youngsters arrive from Douarnenez, and are allocated different islands where they live a Spartan existence either under canvas or in one of the old forts.

On the largest of the Islands (Ile de St-Nicolas) there are fishermen's cottages and a hotel/bar. It comes as something of a surprise to see a public telephone in such a remote spot. Of the two popular anchorages in the Glénans, Ile de Penfret is the easiest approach (from the North). A visiting yacht simply sails towards the prominent lighthouse and then anchors West of the island, where there is a landing slip and a few moorings belonging to the Centre Nautiques des Glénans. This anchorage is well-protected from the East. There is nothing on the island except for the light and a wind-driven generator.The other anchorage, with better protection and nearer to civilisation, is in La Chambre, to the South of St Nicolas. There are also some CNG moorings to the North of Ile de St Nicolas, off the low-tide sandy beach that links St Nicolas to Bananec.

Port la Forêt

Back again on the coast, and still only 20 miles from Pointe de Penmarch, is the Baie de la Forêt. Just inside the Bay, on the West side, is the holiday resort of Beg-Meil. Dinghy sailing is popular off the two fine beaches, and, for larger craft, there are many moorings open only to the East. At the head of the bay is Port la Forêt where there is a fine marina on the East side of Rivière de la Forêt-Fouesnant. In the narrow entrance to the river are two splendid beaches, Cap Coz to port on entering and Kerleven to starboard. The river was once navigable as far as the town of Fouesnant which is 5km inland from the marina.

Concarneau

On the East side of the Baie de la Forêt is the important fishing harbour of Concarneau where large fishing boats leave and enter at all hours of the day and night. Although this is very much a working port, yachts are well provided for in the Avant Port, most of which has been converted into a yacht harbour. Concarneau was one of the most Southerly places to be hit by the great storm in 1987 that tracked up from Biscay, through Northern France, to the South of England. Virtually all the marina in the Avant Port was wiped out. With typical French enthusiasm, the pontoons were soon replaced, and the town once again became a popular passage-harbour for yachts making their way South.

Concarneau is yet another of the towns fortified by Vauban. Overlooking the Avant Port and guarding the entrance to the commercial port, is the Ville Close (walled city). This one-time island now connected to the 'mainland' by a bridge, is still almost encircled by water and by the ramparts above. The Ville Close is now a miniature town, with narrow cobbled streets and old leaning houses that are mostly souvenir shops or art galleries.

The next big harbour along the coast is Lorient which, with offshore Ile de Groix, is in the Morbihan Département which comes outside the scope of this book. Between Concarneau and Lorient are several small fishing harbours. These are not much used by visiting yachts with the exception of Port Manech and the Rivers Belon and Aven. Port Manech, standing at the head of the Aven River, is a delightful, small holiday resort with a drying harbour that may make owners of fin keeled craft wish that they had twin keels. It gets very crowded in the deep-water off the harbour, and many will choose instead to continue up this beautiful river to moor in the deep-water pools at Port l'Hermite or Rosbras (enquire locally if there is enough water to stay afloat). At high water, it is possible to reach Pont-Aven, a favourite haunt of artists, including Gaugan. The Belon river is equally attractive, but much of the water covers oyster beds, around which are a few moorings.

Beyond Finistère's boundary, and just to whet the appetite for continuing South, there is the Ile de Groix which is a useful passage harbour. Then comes the Quiberon Peninsula with marinas at Port Haliguen and La Trinité which is another major yachting centre. The Morbihan (or inland sea) is an area of about 50 square miles of water, dotted with many islands (but first read up about the tides in the pilot books). The inland towns of Vannes and Auray, at the top ends of two of the Morbihan's rivers, are well worth visiting.

Out to sea are three islands, which are great favourites of the author. The main one is Belle Ile, with three remarkably contrasting 'ports'. Le Palais is the island's main harbour with an Avant-Port and a *bassin-à-flot* overlooked by great Vauban fortifications. Then there is Sauzon with

67

deep-water moorings off this charming, colourful fishing harbour. And, again in total contrast, there is an amazing fjord at Stêr Ouen, on the Atlantic side of Belle Ile. Having explored Belle Ile by boat and bicycle, the cruise would be incomplete without visiting the neighbouring small islands of Houat and Hoedic.

Still within this marvellous cruising ground is the large marina development just outside the Morbihan at Le Crouesty. A few miles further along the coast is the Vilaine River where, inland of the barrage, are sheltered moorings and marinas in beautiful surroundings off La Roche Bernard. Then comes the colourful, drying fishing port of Le Croisic (with many deep-water moorings in a large pool off the drying basins). And what about calling in at the up-market resort of La Baule, which has its own yacht harbour at Pornichet? From there, the Loire estuary beckons, along with the holiday resort of Pornic which has a large marina. And the distance between the Pointe de Penmarch and this southern boundary of Brittany? Less than 100 miles!

3 Channel East

Calvados
Honfleur – Deauville – Dives-sur-Mer – Ouistreham – Caen –
Courseulles-sur-Mer – Port-en-Bessin – Grandcamp-Maisy – Isigny

Cross-channel Port: Ouistreham

The coastline of Calvados extends between Honfleur to the East and
Isigny to the West. It is a uniformly flat coastline, with dunes and long
stretches of flat sandy beaches that extend some way off.

This is the area of the June 6th, 1944 D-Day landings, and almost
everywhere ashore are reminders of this piece of history that took place
almost 50 years ago. Apart from the many museums and *Places of
Remembrance*, there are the remains of the German defences in the form
of gun emplacements and bunkers.

It is certainly a good stretch of coastline for yacht harbours with, to
the East of Ouistreham's ferry terminal, the delightful, though crowded
Honfleur in the Seine estuary, the fashionable Deauville and Port
Guillaume at Dives-sur-Mer. To the West is Courseulles-sur-Mer and
Grandcamp-Maisy. Inland from Ouistreham, at the top end of the canal,
is Caen, capital town of the Calvados Département.

Ouistreham and Caen

Unlike the other Channel ferry ports considered in this book, there are
waiting lists for permanent berths at both Ouistreham and Caen, but with
prior agreement it is possible to leave a yacht for several weeks in either
of these yacht basins. The monthly rates are very reasonable, although
they are increased in July and August (even over this peak period the
rates compare well with those on the South coast of England). The
monthly *tarif* for October – May is considerably reduced, and boat
owners could consider Ouistreham, with excellent facilities ashore, as a
place in which to lay up for the winter months.

Typical of this stretch of coastline, the sandbanks off Ouistreham
extend to about a mile offshore. The approach channel here has to be
dredged regularly to maintain sufficient depth at low water springs to
take the cross-channel ferries, which berth just outside the locks.

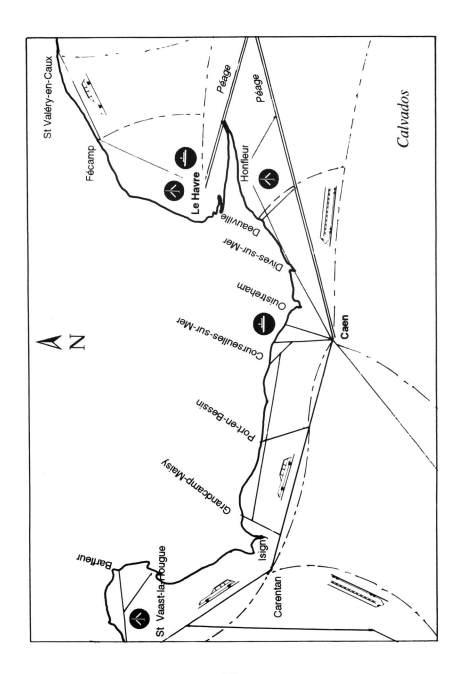

The channel is well marked with prominent port and starboard beacons that start some way offshore. The only difficulty might be locating the seaward pillar buoy, because the coastline here is uniformly flat to the West of the entrance, and only slightly higher to the East. Sight of the 37m high lighthouse (to port on entering), should confirm the location of the entrance some way off. One of the leading lights here has a range of 22 miles, and can sometimes be useful during the day if the visibility is murky.

To the East of the entrance is the estuary of the Orne where, at Mereville-Franceville, there are many drying moorings including 50 places for visiting yachts that can take the ground conveniently. To the West is Riva-Bella, with its long beach lined with bathing huts. Ouistreham and Riva-Bella together make up a popular holiday resort, with many shops in the centre of the town catering for tourists.

There are two locks into the Ouistreham-Caen canal. The West side lock is the newer one, built to take ships. The smaller lock to the East is the one used by yachts. The gates are worked for 3 hours before and after high water between 0600hrs and 2200hrs. The yacht harbour, belonging to the local *Chambre de Commerce*, is immediately to port, having passed through the lock. There are 650 berths here, but 70% of these are permanently let. This 70% cannot be varied, and when one of the permanent berths does come free it is offered to the boat owner at the top of the list of the other 30% who pay considerably more for their annual rental (and there is a two-year waiting list simply to be accommodated as one of the 30%).

There is a lively yacht club here, with a clubhouse that has a library and where TV can be watched. Other shore-based activities at Ouistreham-Riva Bella include karting, pony club, and there is a centre for sea water cures (thalassotherapeutical). On the East side of the Arrière port is a drying quay for the fishing fleet with nearby fish stalls. (You do not have to look far to find the accompanying *frites*.) If a boat owner wants to proceed up the canal to Caen, then a visit to the Capitainerie at Ouistreham is recommended to establish the opening times of the bridges and pay the canal dues.

It takes about 1½ – 2 hours to motor the 16km from Ouistreham to Caen. This can involve short delays while waiting for one of the four lifting bridges to open. There is also a viaduct (33m high) spanning the canal. The first of the lifting bridges, 5km from Ouistreham, is the site of the famous Pegasus bridge that was the scene of fierce fighting in 1944.

The Port de Caen is in the city centre, with yacht pontoons in the Bassin St-Pierre. Caen was founded by William the Conqueror and his wife Mathilde who was Princess of Flanders, Belgium and Normandy. Many of the buildings were destroyed in the war, but two fine 11th-century Abbeys remain. The Abbaye des Hommes was built by William, and the Abbaye aux Dames was built by Mathilde to appease the Pope, who was greatly upset by their marriage. As cousins, William and Mathilde were too closely related for their marriage to be considered proper. There is also much remaining of the ramparts of Caen Castle, built by William when he decided to make Caen his capital.

Caen is a pleasing mix of modern office blocks along with traditional architecture, representing what had been before. There are many parks and gardens and Caen is considered one of the *greenest* towns in France.

Dives-sur-Mer

Just 6 miles to the East of Ouistreham is the entrance to the drying Dives River. Not all that many years ago, the Dives and the holiday resort of Cabourg warranted no more than 2 or 3 lines in the cruising guides of the area. The shifting sandbanks off the entrance were sparsely marked, and the members of the Cabourg Yacht Club virtually had the place to themselves.

Port Guillaume was officially inaugurated on 15th June, 1991. The 'port' now consists of a new yacht basin at Dives-sur-Mer, the drying river moorings off Dives and Cabourg, and a quay (mostly used by fishing boats) at Houlgate in the entrance to the river. The yacht basin, which has excellent facilities and plenty of room for visitors, is 1.5 miles from the first of the channel buoys. The single gate stays open day and night when there is 2m or more over the sill. (Approximately 6-6½ hours each tide.)

The new yacht harbour is a good example of the local Chamber of Commerce and the Regional Authority working alongside property developers. The plan was conceived on the initiative of the Conseil General of Calvados at a time when there was considerable unemployment locally as a result of the closure of a large factory on the South side of the Dives River. By providing alternative employment and a boost to the local tourist industry, the creation of Port Guillaume seemed the ideal solution.

The development plan, including the yacht harbour, covers an area of about 50 acres of what was originally waste land. The plan allows for a

Port Guillaume, Dives-sur-Mer

new community with their own houses, apartments, shops and restaurants. There will also be parkland and a recreational centre. Inevitably, this will mean that for a year or two the area around the yacht basin will take on the appearance of a large building site. The author's view is that the delightful surroundings here will more than offset the temporary view of cranes, JCBs and scaffolding.

Dives, like several one-time ports along this stretch of the coastline, is now 2km inland. Before the gradual silting up of the river, Dives was an important deep-water port where, in 1066 William the Conqueror assembled an army of 15,000 men and 696 ships to invade England; the precise spot from which William set sail is marked by the Salle de Départ.

For three centuries, the *Village de Guillaume le Conquerant* in the centre of Dives, was an important staging post. The *Village* today consists of the original *hostellerie*, and a tiny square and courtyard surrounded by beautifully restored houses where Dives craftsmen and artists display their products. Dives has a covered market, which dates back to the 14th and 15th Centuries. The market takes place here on Saturday mornings beneath huge timber frames supporting a roof that almost touches the ground. Another remarkable building is Notre-Dame-de-Dives, a 14th-15th century church, reflecting the one-time importance of what had been a major port.

Dives is actually wedged between two flourishing holiday resorts, Cabourg to the West and Houlgate to the East. As part of the development plan of Port Guillaume, Dives is now linked to Cabourg by means of a footbridge over the river. As a result, the long beach with its bathing tents and promenade can be reached in a 10 minute stroll from the yacht harbour. Also at Cabourg is a casino, the imposing Pullman Hotel, together with many shops and restaurants.

Neighbouring Houlgate is by no means a poor relation to Cabourg. The fishing harbour, to port on entering the Dives River, is about 200m from the Capitainerie. Beyond the fishing quay is the resort proper, with a superb beach, along with the resort's casino and Sporting Club. There are several top-rated hotels and tree-lined avenues behind which are many secluded villas.

Deauville and Trouville

7 miles to the North-East of Dives, is the exclusive resort of Deauville. There was a time when, during the short season from mid-July to the end of August, one went there to see and be seen, rubbing shoulders with royalty and millionaires strolling along the famous 'Planches' or wooden promenade, with grand hotels like the famous Hotel Normandy to one side and the impeccably clean beach with its gaudy bathing tents on the other. The season at Deauville has now been extended into September by their annual film festival, which is second only to Cannes. There remain many pursuits here for the wealthy such as horse racing, polo, golf, tennis, dressage and show jumping, and, of course, gambling at what some claim to be the most exclusive casino in the world.

It is also a yachting playground, where Dragons are hauled out of the water between races to be lovingly polished. The annual Cowes – Deauville race is an important event in the yacht racing calendar. This takes place in May, attracting an entry well in excess of a hundred boats, many of whom will finish up crammed into the municipal yacht harbour.

There are actually two yacht harbours in Deauville – the Port

Deauville Marina

Municipal and Port Deauville which is a private development; both make provision for visiting yachts, of which about a third are British. The facilities for yachts visiting Port Deauville are strictly limited, as many of the berth holders also have a waterside-apartment here. There is a bar, a Crêperie and a small shop selling basic provisions. The Deauville Yacht Club overlooks the municipal harbour. All visiting crews are made very welcome here, but it is that much further to walk to and from Port Deauville. The municipal harbour is nearer the town centre and the station. Port Deauville is closer to the *'Promenade des Planches'* and the magnificent sweep of sands said to be one of the largest and most beautiful in Europe. Port Deauville, where the overnight *tarif* is more expensive, resembles one of those exclusive London dockland developments where a pontoon berth goes along with an apartment.

One of the advantages of Port Deauville is that the lock is worked whenever there is sufficient water for yachts to cross the extensive drying sandbanks off the entrance. In practice this means that entry to Port Deauville is possible for a boat drawing 1.5m anytime over a period between + or − 4½ hrs HW (neaps) and slightly longer at springs. If making for the municipal harbour, however, the entry times are more restricted with the gates open + or – 2hrs HW.

Trouville, joined by bridge to Deauville, is perhaps overshadowed by its exclusive neighbour. The season is longer at Trouville which is actually the older of the two. It is primarily a fishing port at the entrance to the River Touques with the drying quays packed with colourful fishing boats. There are no facilities here for yachts, but is well worth the walk from Deauville to explore this holiday resort which has its own opulent casino, a long promenade and a *'Hotel de Ville'* that even manages to outshine that of Deauville. Some of the best restaurants in the vicinity, along with wonderful wine cellars can be found in the maze of ancient side streets. There is a daily market here, and, down by the quayside, is an ancient fish market. Large working boats are still constructed at Trouville.

Honfleur

Honfleur, the most Easterly port in the Calvados Département, is just over 20 miles from Ouistreham. Much-favoured by painters and photographers, this small harbour also attracts many visiting yachts, a large proportion of which are British. The port is also used by small coasters and fishing boats who have their own basin (Bassin de l'Est).

Situated on the West side of the estuary to the River Seine, the approach to Honfleur from the main deep water shipping channel, is over banks of mud, unlike the other Calvados harbours with their offlying sandbanks. During the season, the basin gates are worked from HW-1 to HW +3. Over this four hour period there are 4 openings during the day and 3 openings at night. Yachts arriving off Honfleur around LW can anchor near the entrance to the approach channel and be reasonably out of the tide, nudging further and further in as the water rises. The long sea wall (to starboard on entering) is where locals and visitors take their evening stroll beneath the trees.

Once inside the Vieux Bassin, one can relish the surroundings. Reflected in the water are the cafés, restaurants and gaily coloured houses all packed tightly together. There are many old buildings here, including the 15th century church of Ste Catherine which was built entirely of wood by local boat builders. Curiously, the church's belfry was built on the other side of the square.

Anyone interested in impressionist paintings will have the opportunity to see retrospective shows during March, April and May by Jean Boudin, who was a local artist. Other notables, whose works are displayed in

Honfleur

Honfleur, include Monet who produced many paintings of the Seine and its surroundings. There are art galleries galore, many selling modern paintings of local scenes.

Unfortunately one cannot be too euphoric these days about Honfleur. Much of the Vieux Bassin is taken up with local boats pointing their bows towards the quayside, and each with the stern rope attached to individual mooring buoys. In the South-West corner of the yacht basin is a pontoon with space alongside for three visiting yachts.

In July and August, the place throngs with visitors as does the yacht basin. Each of the yachts alongside the pontoon may well be joined with a dozen or so more, ranged up alongside, and extending right out to the middle of the basin. In an unsuccessful attempt to combat this overcrowding, the maximum stay for any visiting yacht is a week. There is a yacht club here, who are helpful with local advice, but the premises, which overlook the basin, are really for locals only and have limited opening times.

Courseulles

To the West of Ouistreham, and still in Calvados, are four harbours: Courseulles-sur-Mer, Port-en-Bessin, Grandcamp-Maisy and Isigny. Like most of the harbours in this part of Normandy, Courseulles is reached by a dredged channel running through sandbanks that extend almost a mile offshore. Typically, the entrance here is difficult to locate from some way out during daylight hours. There are no easily identifiable landmarks (there are several church spires, but it is difficult to establish which is which on the chart). The navigator may have to settle for locating the single buoy over a mile off Courseulles, and use this to set a safe course towards the entrance channel. Closer in, there are more marks, and there is no mistaking the end of the wooden pierhead which is left to port on entering, with a prominent Crucifix to starboard. There are two wet basins exclusively for yachts. The Nouveau Bassin which is hard to starboard having passed through the drying Avant Port, is primarily for private use. There is a sill here with a swing bridge. Entry is possible for 2½ hours either side of high water for yachts drawing up to 1.2m. There are 500 pontoon berths in this new basin, some of which have been leased to be combined with the somewhat out-of-place blocks of apartments that overlook the yachts.

Visiting yachts continue up to the top end of the Avant Port, through the gates (with lifting bridge) and into the Basin Joinville. The lock gates are worked two hours either side of HW. The capacity of Basin Joinville is 220 yachts, including visitors, and there is a waiting list here for permanent berths. Strangely enough, the cost of a night stay here is more than a visitor pays for a berth in the municipal harbour at Deauville.

There is a yacht club (Société des Régates de Courseulles) with an attractive and hospitable Clubhouse on the Quai Est. There is also an active sailing school, and many races are organised by SRC. It is very much a holiday resort, with a fine beach and a two-star camping site.

Courseulles is particularly noted for its oyster beds and coquillages. This industry goes back to the beginning of the nineteenth century when vast numbers of oysters and coquilles Saint-Jacques were transported to the Paris markets to finish up as part of the menu of the city's more expensive restaurants. There is the *Maison de la Mer* at Courseulles, which is an aquarium, an exhibition of the way oysters are cultivated, and a museum devoted exclusively to shell-fish.

Port-en-Bassin

The next harbour, westwards along the coast, is Port-en-Bessin, which is 12 miles from Courseulles. It is debatable whether the pilots of the area should include detailed instructions on how to enter this important fishing harbour. Some would say that yachts should be discouraged, leaving the place to the large fishing fleet. It is a difficult place to enter in winds between North-East and North-West. A good number of boats choose to remain in the Avant Port, where they dry out. The lock gate opens for two hours either side of high water. This does not allow entry until the swing bridge is operated, which is at infrequent intervals to meet the movements in and out of harbour of the fishing fleet. Once through the entrance to the deep water basins, visiting yachts are expected to berth on the quayside immediately to starboard. The fishing fleet have the exclusive use of the inner basin where they unload the catch by the fish market.

Grandcamp-Maisy

Back again to the Calvados yacht harbours and the popular holiday and sailing resorts, Grandcamp-Maisy is 12 miles West of Port-en-Bessin. There is one significant difference between Grandcamp and the other yacht harbours along the coastline, all of which have dredged channels through sandbanks extending about a mile offshore. Entering or leaving Grandcamp-Maisy means crossing over a ledge of rock – the drying Roches de Grandcamp – which extend right across the entrance to the harbour and about 2 miles either side. Providing there is not an onshore wind, the rocky shelf can the crossed + or – 2hrs (springs) or + or – 1½hrs (neaps).The plateau of rock is flat, so providing there is sufficient water, the approach course is not critical. The lock gates at Grandcamp are worked between HW – 2 and HW + 2½, so having timed the passage to cross the offlying *roches*, a yacht should be able to pass through the lock with little delay. Visiting yachts have individual finger berths towards the end of the first East – West pontoon, which is to starboard on entering. When these are full, visitors raft up on the ends of both pontoons. The quaysides are reserved for fishing boats. The harbour master's office, where there are showers, is on the South-West corner of the harbour, right next to the fish market.

Grandcamp-Maisy is a small, unpretentious holiday resort. *'Promenades en Mer'* are a local attraction, aboard the *vedette* 'Colonel Rudder' which can take 65 passengers and is equipped with a bar. There are fishing parties, trips to the Iles Saint-Marcouf (see chapter on the

Manche harbours), or a tour of the nearby Plage du Débarquement (the West end of Omaha beach). There are also boat excursions to the Pointe du Hoc. Here, little has been done to disturb the remains of the furious battle with which Omaha is associated. The shell holes, gun batteries and bunkers, remain untouched, serving as a grim reminder of the appalling losses suffered here.

Isigny

The most westerly harbour in Calvados is Isigny, although the place hardly justifies being included as a yacht harbour. Isigny, with the neighbouring harbour of Carentan (see Manche chapter) are situated in the Baie du Grand Vey where the sandbanks are constantly on the move. The drying Isigny channel is conspicuously marked with buoys, but these should be treated as a guide only. Ideally, entering or leaving Isigny should be timed so that the passage over the Baie du Grand Vey is made on a rising tide. It is a distance of about 4 miles from the first of the Isigny channel buoys (to seaward of the Roches de Grandcamp) to the sunken breakwaters marking the entrance to the River Aure. Thence it is about another ½ mile to the town of Isigny. There are pontoons on the starboard side when approaching, but these are some distance from the town. All the berths (including the pontoon) at Isigny dry out, and care should be taken to make sure the boat stays upright in the mud, avoiding falling over where it shelves, as it does towards the centre of the channel.

This is the heart of the lush green pastures of the Bessin region, associated with dairy produce for which Isigny is world famous.

> ## Seine-Maritime
> Le Havre – Fécamp – St Valéry-en-Caux – Dieppe – Le Tréport –
> Rouen – Paris

Cross-channel Ports: Le Havre, Dieppe

The coastline of the Seine-Maritime Département runs from Le Havre, on the North side of the Seine estuary, to Le Tréport and the regional boundary between Normandy and Picardy. This is a coastline of towering chalk cliffs and pebbly beaches, in stark contrast to the Calvados coastline to the South-West of the Seine.

The owner of a yacht based in the marina at Le Havre has an interesting and varied choice of places to visit in the Seine-Maritime Département. To the North-East is Fécamp, St Valéry-en-Caux, Dieppe (which may become an important yachting harbour) and Le Tréport, where there is already a major development well underway which will attract many visiting yachts. An alternative, and still in the Seine-Maritime as far as Rouen, is a cruise up the River Seine, and then continue beyond Rouen along the canalised Seine to Paris. The other possibility is to sail westwards to the Calvados harbours previously described.

Le Havre

Le Havre is France's second port, founded in 1509 by King Francois the First as an alternative to nearby Harfleur and Honfleur which had silted up. It comes as something of a surprise when visited for the first time; the entire city seems to be all great concrete blocks of uniformly grey offices and apartments.

Of all the cities in France, Le Havre suffered the most bomb damage in the last war. The priority after the war was to rebuild the city as soon as possible. There would be no attempt to reproduce what had been before (like St Malo for example). The city commissioned Auguste Perret, who was from the new school of architects preferring reinforced concrete, to come up with an overall plan. The result was a city unlike anything that the French had seen before. The buildings are high, the roads are straight and wide, and in the centre is the *Place de l'Hôtel-de-Ville*, one of the largest city squares in Europe.

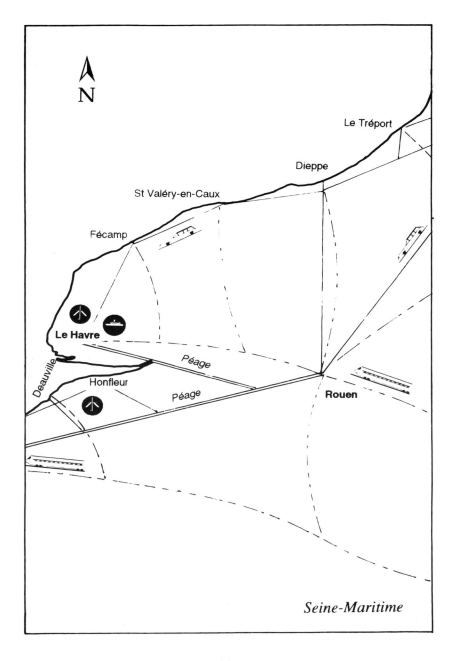

In amongst all the concrete of Le Havre are some remarkable modern buildings like St Joseph's Church – glass with a tower block for a spire; the Town Hall with an indoor garden below ground level; the André Malraux Musée des Beaux-Arts on the seafront which has a superb collection of Impressionist paintings; the Oscar Niemeyer House of Culture with galleries and a theatre all housed beneath what looks like a giant cooling tower, with a baby one alongside. One or two original buildings survived World War II, including Notre-Dame Cathedral and the 17th century Musée de l'Ancien Havre which is near the Bassin du Commerce in the old St Francois quarter.

To the North of the city, is a tunnel exit, used by cars, cyclists and walkers making for the Fôret de Montgeon. This green suburb of Le Havre has a boating lake, a golf course, an ice rink and a sports stadium.

Anyone wanting to see the lower Seine in style, can embark from Le Havre on the *Salamandre* or the *River's King*, cruising up river as far as Rouen, with occasional sailings all the way up to Paris. These vedettes have a dining room, a bar and even a disco on one of them.

Le Havre port operates a 'warm berth' turnaround at the ferry terminal, when almost as soon as one ferry has departed another takes its place. This should not be a problem for yachts arriving or leaving Le Havre, because there is a vast Avant Port, entered at any time, from either the West or the South. The Port de Plaisance, right over on the West side of the Avant Port, is isolated from the main commercial port with its ferry terminal, locks and basins.

In 1985, a new wall was completed in the entrance to the marina. The capacity was then increased to 1,100 berths. This total is accommodated in two sections of the marina – the outer pontoons take 800 boats (5–12m), and the inner 300 boats (7–18m). There are 50 visitors' berths in the outer and 20–25 in the inner.

The Port de Plaisance is conveniently close to the town centre and also to a reasonable bathing beach (all pebbles except around low water). Facing the Port de Plaisance, is the *Boulevard Clémenceau*. An interesting development has started here, with a plan to make the Boulevard into a Promenade. This will be flanked by gardens, trees and a boating lake. The situation and the outlook from the Port de Plaisance will be greatly enhanced. As part of this general development, it is planned to move the fishing boats from their berths in the Port de Plaisance, making room for a total of 1,300 places for yachts. The whole project is scheduled for completion 1993/94.

Apart from the roll-on/roll-off ferry services, this one-time port of the famous liners, is much used by giant container ships and by oil tankers, making for the local refineries. There is, as one would expect, a well-marked but narrow deep water channel into the Seine estuary. The first mark is about 10 miles out, and shipping must stay in the channel because there are many sand banks in the entrance to the Seine.

Just in the Seine estuary, on the North side, is the Ville de Sainte-Adresse. This is really a suburb of Le Havre, and from a sailing point of view has little to offer cruising boats. Instead, Sainte-Adresse has built up a reputation for serious windsurfing, organising many international windsurfing events throughout the year.

To the North of Le Havre, the steep chalk cliffs dominate virtually the entire 70-mile coastline of the Seine-Maritime. The few gaps in the chalk face, mark the position of either a holiday resort or one of the Channel ports. The first gap, just 10 miles to the North of Le Havre, is Port d'Antifer. This is exclusively for oil tankers, accommodating vessels of up to 500,000 tons. There is a well-marked channel into Antifer, with the outside buoys about 12 miles offshore. The channel runs NW/SE, and yachts must exercise some caution in this area because these giant tankers can hardly be expected to alter their course or speed.

The next gap in the chalk cliffs, 15 miles to the North, is the holiday resort of Etretat. There is little in the way of boats here, apart from a few fishing boats, drawn up on the shingle beach, and the usual collection of windsurfers. There is a fine promenade here and the almost inevitable casino. The remarkably shaped cliffs, either side of Etretat, are featured on many postcards and on much of the local Département tourist literature. At one end of Etretat's beach is the Porte d'Aval, with Porte d'Amant on the other. 'Porte' here refers to a spectacular 'doorway' driven into the chalk face by the sea. There are good walks along cliff-top pathways; those with no head for heights can stride purposefully along the promenade, taking in the therapy of ozone and iodine for which the resort is famous.

Fécamp

Fécamp, 24 miles from Le Havre, is only 76 miles from the Nab Tower in the Eastern approaches to the Solent. The distance to Le Havre from Nab is actually more (84). Fécamp is even closer to Brighton (68), so it is hardly surprising that this one-time great fishing port receives a good number of visiting English yachts (most years it is around 900 for the season). Fécamp is in its own valley that meets the sea between towering, perpendicular cliffs of which Cap Fagnet to the North is the highest in

Fécamp

Normandy. For the energetic there are more spectacular cliff-top walks here.

The entrance to Fécamp is straight forward, presenting no problems except around low water when there is a minimum of 1.5m in the entrance. Low water combined with strong W/NW winds can kick up a dangerous sea when it would be prudent to postpone entry until an hour before high water.

The deep water marina at Fécamp (to starboard on entering) has 530 berths of which 30 are for visitors. If the place is overcrowded or the strong winds from the West produce a swell that rebounds into the marina, making it uncomfortable, then it may be preferable to make for the pontoons in the Bassin Berigny which opens for about two hours before high water (a shorter duration at neaps). There is a project at Fécamp, scheduled for completion in 1993, to provide in the Bassin Berigny an additional 250 pontoon berths, of which 35 will be for visitors. Opening hours of the Bassin will be extended to HW + or -2. At the present time (1992) it is considerably cheaper to use the basin for a night or two, compared with the Avant Port.

The pontoons in the Avant Port run out from the Quai Vauban where there is an impressive star-shaped building, with views in every direction. This houses both the *Capitainerie* and the *Société des Régates de Fécamp*. To the South of the harbour entrance is the resort's modest beach which, in season, is packed with holiday-makers. There is a short promenade here lined with bathing huts. Undoubtedly Fécamp's main tourist attraction is a visit to the *Palais*, where the world-famous Bénédictine liquor is produced. The blend, which dates back to the 16th century, was originally made up by the local monks, who collected a variety of plants from the cliff tops. The *Palais Bénédictine* houses the copper stills and oak casks in which this mix of 27 plants and herbs is matured and blended. The *Palais* also has a museum exhibiting, in an imposing and beautifully furnished and decorated room, collections from the old abbey and monastery. At the end of the tour of the Palace, visitors are invited to sample their famous product.

St-Valéry-en-Caux

Roughly half-way between Fécamp and Dieppe is the yachting centre of St-Valéry-en-Caux. The approach is very similar to that of Fécamp – making for the only gap in the cliffs where, at the head of a ravine, lies this holiday resort with its fine beach. The entrance to the Port de Plaisance is through a lifting bridge and gates that open + or − 2¼ hrs HW. The Avant Port dries, and in strong winds from the W − NE care should be taken to avoid entering the Avant Port too early, when the approach may be distinctly choppy.

The yacht basin accommodates nearly 600 craft. It is right in the centre of the old part of St-Valéry-en-Caux with many shops just a short walk from the town quays.

Dieppe

Dieppe comes as something of a surprise to those who might have dismissed it as a ferry terminal, with the shops and restaurants catering mainly for the English day-tripper. Many large hotels and the casino overlook the town's fine, wide, long beach and promenade, at the ends of which are the familiar chalk cliffs of the Seine-Maritime coastline. The old quarter of Dieppe is a lively, labyrinth of narrow streets packed with bars, restaurants and interesting shops. Many buildings survived World War ll, including the imposing castle overlooking the beach.

The premises of Dieppe's yacht club look out across the *Avant Port*. There are some pontoons, provided by club members, positioned in front of the club house. Prior to 1992, these pontoons could be uncomfortable

Dieppe

particularly if the wind was between North-East and North-West. From early 1992, a 300m extension to the western breakwater has provided all round protection in the Avant Port. Yachts also use these pontoons if waiting to enter the Bassin Duquesne (*bassin-à-flot*). Access into the basin is through a gate and lifting bridge worked -2 +1HW. There are more club pontoons in the Bassin Duquesne, providing berths for about 70 boats near the centre of the town.

There is a large re-development plan for Dieppe, some of which is already under way. The plan provides for a new ferry terminal in the outer harbour, relocation of the commercial and fishing harbours, and two new marinas. The first, scheduled for completion in 93/94, uses the Quai Henri IV in the Avant Port. Towards the end of the town's 5 year plan, a second marina will be provided in the Bassin Duquesne. Dieppe is certainly worth watching, for this not unattractive holiday resort may well become a yachting centre.

Le Tréport

The most easterly of the Seine-Maritime's ports is Le Tréport. Like Dieppe, this too is worth watching since they have a £15 million project underway to develop both the commercial and fishing harbours and to

Eu

create a Port de Plaisance. A new lock is completed, providing the fishing boats access to their new quays. There are also temporary finger berths for yachts in the new fishing port, prior to completion of the Port de Plaisance.

In 1991, a visitor to Le Tréport would have wondered why there was little more than a handful of yachts based at this lively holiday resort which attracts many visitors from Paris. The harbour consisted of a drying Avant Port and a lock giving access to the Port de Commerce. Many years earlier, Le Tréport was linked to the town of Eu by a canal. Eu, now 1½ miles from the sea, was then an important commercial port.

Beyond the new lock, at the far end of the fishing port, is the site for the 320 berth Port de Plaisance. By removing a low bridge, craft in the yacht harbour will have access to the Le Tréport-Eu canal (minimum depth 3m).

Once again, large sailing boats will be seen by the tow path as they were a hundred years ago. Craft with a height above waterline in excess of 6 metres cannot reach Eu, because of a new motorway bridge (the A16 to Paris). Boats with fixed masts can, however, cover ⅔rds of the distance to the town, and still enjoy what might be a new experience to some boat owners – mooring in the peace of the countryside, surrounded by trees and lush meadows. From here it is only about 10-15 minutes walk along the tow-path to what used to be the ancient port of Eu. The canal finishes here, widening out into a pool where the sailing ships used to turn. There is still a *Quai Maritime* here and a *Café de la Marine* serving as a reminder of what had been at the turn of the Century.

The elegant town of Eu is dominated by the Gothic church of Notre-Dame-et-St-Laurent O'Toole (after an Irish Primate who spent his latter years here). To the West of the town, surrounded by trees and lawns, is the magnificent Château d'Eu. Queen Victoria and Prince Albert stayed here when it was the summer residence of King Louis-Philippe. Completion of the *Châmbre de Commerce*'s ambitious project is planned for 1993 to coincide with the 150th year of the canal.

The River Seine
Le Havre – Rouen – Paris

Any owner, who has based the boat at Le Havre, is admirably placed for a Seine cruise to Paris. For many, this inland waterway cruising, will be a new experience with the bonus of being in the centre of Paris a few days after leaving Le Havre. It is actually possible, given good progress through the locks above Rouen and early starts, to reach the capital city in 5 days. Those who choose to enjoy the many delightful distractions en route, should allow at least a full week.

Paris, as the crow flies, is roughly 200 kms from Le Havre. By the Seine it is a distance of 368 km which includes 6 locks upriver of Rouen. Apart from the suburbs of Rouen and Paris, the Seine meanders through delightful countryside. On one side there may be woods and chalk cliffs and on the other green fields as far as the eye can see.

If contemplating a Seine-cruise, the first consideration is the height of the boat above waterline (*tirant d'air*). There is no limit between Rouen and the sea, but above Rouen where the low bridges come thick and fast, the *tirant d'air* varies depending on the height of the non-tidal river and which particular section is being navigated. Condensing this information, between Rouen and Paris the maximum permitted height of a boat is 6.0m in normal river conditions, dropping to 3.7m if the water level of the river is exceptionally high due to flooding.

The limit in draught (*tirant d'eau*) or width is hardly relevant because pleasure craft will be sharing the waters of the non-tidal upper Seine with massive barges or *péniches*.

A yacht with a fixed mast can have this removed and stowed at Le Havre or at Rouen. Le Havre is mostly used, and is the obvious choice for yachts based here, as this operation can be carried out prior to the owner joining the boat (yet again, the cost of removing, storage and stepping, is considerably less at Le Havre than it would be at a boat yard on the UK's South coast.) A yacht arriving at Rouen, still with fixed mast, should be secured to the pontoon in St-Gervais basin (not the most salubrious surroundings) where a crane is available. The basin is to port downstream of the centre of Rouen, just before kilometre post 245. Permission to use the pontoon and crane must be sought from the Harbour Master. The operation takes more organising in Rouen compared with Le Havre, and actually achieves little, because sailing is not encouraged on the Seine. Anyone who tried sailing in the lower reaches, would find it frustrating; the wind is either blanketed or continually heading the boat, following the sweep of the river, and it is essential to maintain at least 5 knots through the water to reach Rouen on the one tide.

Leaving Le Havre, to cross the Seine estuary, wind against tide conditions can make the passage extremely uncomfortable. Being out at sea will be a strange experience for those on board sailing yachts, which have been temporarily converted to motor boats. The Seine estuary is no place to get caught, particularly in a strong blow from the SW. There are several drying sandbanks, which the pilot books will tell you are constantly on the move. The channel in the estuary is surprisingly narrow and much-used by shipping plying between the sea and Rouen.

The strong tides of the Seine estuary can be avoided by making use of the Tankerville Canal. This 25km waterway, with locks at either end, is entered at Le Havre and comes out just below the giant Tankerville suspension bridge. Yachts making for the entrance to the canal from the yacht harbour may be delayed by the additional locks and lifting bridges to be negotiated to pass through Le Havre's commercial port. The canal traffic is heavy, and pleasure boats are hardly encouraged to use this waterway to bypass just a few miles of the estuary. Because of the times the Tancarville locks are operated (HW- 4 to HW+ 3¼), a small boat using the canal will not be able to leave for Rouen at the critical time to complete the passage on one tide (see below).

Tides are complex in the lower Seine. Some basic facts – high water in Rouen is roughly 6 hours after high water in the Seine estuary. There is a long stand around high water at both Rouen and at le Havre. In the estuary of the Seine and off Honfleur, there is a 3 knot tide at springs.

River Seine

This increases to 4 knots as the river narrows, and for another 45km up as far as Caudebec. The strength of the tide between Caudebec and Rouen gradually decreases to 3 knots at springs (1.5 knots neaps). The dreaded Mascaret (similar to the Seven Bore) is fortunately something from the past. Under certain conditions, this huge tidal wave rushed up the narrows of the Seine at around 12 knots. It only happened when there were exceptionally high tides at Le Havre. These days the Mascaret has been tamed by dredging and by constructing training walls in the estuary. Even now, on exceptionally high tides, a wave builds up at the beginning of the flood, between Quillebeuf and La Mailleraye. In this 30km stretch, for a minute or two, just after local low water, there can be a rush of water reaching about ten knots. Years ago, the town of Caudebec, on this section of river, drew many visitors over the autumn equinoctial tides to witness the phenomenon. There is a memorial stone here for a young girl who was swept off the bank of the Seine by the mascaret and was drowned.

Starting from Le Havre with the first of the flood, there will be around 10 hours of favourable tide to complete the 130km of river to Rouen; a boat with a modest 8hp engine, able to motor at about 5 knots through the water, will be able to make Rouen on one extended tide. The navigator is not redundant, as progress towards Rouen can be plotted from the posts on the river bank which mark every kilometre between Paris and Honfleur.

The same craft, making the return trip back to Le Havre will leave Rouen around HW. After about 4 hours, she will start to feel the advancing flood tide; instead of flogging a foul tide for a few hours, most crews choose to pick up a mooring or anchor to await the approach of local high tide, after which the passage can be resumed. This return trip will take a small yacht about 14 hours to complete, and must be carefully planned to make certain the boat is not still underway after sunset (pleasure boats are strictly forbidden to be underway in the tidal Seine over the period of 30 minutes after sunset to 30 minutes before sunrise).

On the way up to Rouen, the crew should be looking out for possible stopping off places on the return trip to Le Havre. The choice of anchorages or unoccupied moorings is strictly limited. The commercial traffic is on the go both day and night; they produce an uncomfortable wash at the best of times and more so in the straight sections of river, where they increase speed to keep up with a tight schedule. Apart from the wash from passing shipping, there is the strength of the tide to contend with, and not knowing whether the bed of the river is suitable for anchoring. The mooring buoys are mostly for commercial traffic, and, in their own interests, pleasure craft should avoid the temptation to secure alongside a quay, when the wash from passing traffic can cause extensive damage. So, where can a yacht lie to wait for the next high water? Anchoring is possible outside the main channel, perhaps in a protected backwater if there is sufficient water. Duclair is a pleasant waterside village, with its own yacht club, off which there may be a free mooring buoy. There are also moorings at Caudebec.

Having reached Rouen, with the mast lowered, a yacht can continue under the first three of the city's bridges; a one-way traffic system operates through the North end of next bridge to gain access to the *Bras du Pré aux Loups* (left bank of the Seine). Moving along the *Bras du Pré aux Loups* can only be undertaken against the tide. This means that if a yacht arrives at the bridge when the tide is still flooding, it will be necessary to motor on to the South of Ile Lacroix, turning round to skirt the Southern end of the Ile to enter the *Bras du Pré aux Loups* from the South. On the North side of the Ile Lacroix is the boat yard Villetard (the first stopping place to take on fuel after leaving Le Havre). Just beyond are pontoons for visiting yachts in a small marina which has water, electricity and showers.

The pontoon berths are not far from the centre of Rouen. Crews of visiting yachts may want to rest up here to see something of this famous city which is the capital of upper Normandy. Old Rouen, the area of greatest interest, is compact, and can therefore be covered on foot. References to Joan of Arc are much in evidence, particularly in the Place du Vieux-Marché where she was burned at the stake. This old quarter, dominated by the cathedral, is packed with museums contained within fine old buildings, and with galleries filled with priceless paintings.

Leaving the visitors' pontoons to continue towards Paris, the one-way system along the *Bras du Pré aux Loups* must again be observed. There is still something of a flood tide, which runs for about four hours before the local high water, reaching 3 knots at springs. Above Rouen the effects of the tide gradually fade away, to be replaced beyond Elbeuf by the natural down river current which is rarely more than a knot.

The first of the six locks, Amfréville, is 40km from the pontoons at Rouen. (There are actually seven locks between Rouen and Paris, but craft proceeding in either direction can choose whether they use Bougival (49km from Paris) or the smaller Châtou (45km). The Seine locks are vast, accommodating many barges in a single opening. There may be several basins operating, with traffic moving in under the strict control of the lock keeper, who sits in his ivory tower communicating with those waiting to enter by loudspeaker and VHF. The commercial traffic has priority over pleasure craft, who must keep well clear of the manoeuvring barges. It can be slightly difficult for a yacht, because there may be a long queue of barges waiting to enter and, whilst not wishing to appear a queue jumper, it is desirable that the yacht should be seen by the lock keeper. You can find out if there is a wait and which basin to enter by calling the lock keeper on VHF. Channel 18 for Poses-Amfréville, Mericourt, Chëtou; Channel 22 for Notre Dame de la

Garènne, Andrèsy, Bougival, Suresnes. It is sometimes possible to squeeze a small craft into the lock behind the barges. There will then be little turbulence felt when the sluices are opened; the props of the barges getting underway can be more of a problem, and yachts will be unpopular if they hang about too long within the lock to avoid this.

The locks are operated from 0700 – 1900 hrs. Having passed through the first lock, there are no more worries about tide (just a gentle flow of the river), so the choice of night stops is almost limitless. By gently approaching the river bank, it is possible to moor in a quiet section of the river, miles away from anywhere. Anyone who is really pressed for time will continue up river to the next lock to await the 0700 opening. There are many *haltes nautiques* usually around some of the Seine villages. Mostly these consist of little more than a quay reserved for pleasure craft, perhaps showers at a nearby camp site, with a garage, shops, a café and a restaurant close by. These *haltes nautiques* are clearly shown in the Seine Guide referred to below. Some of the larger quays are for barge traffic only. The bargees are a race apart. Many barges are run as family concerns, with the husband the skipper, the wife the mate, and perhaps one or two small children playing in safety pens around the wheelhouse. The barges motor along at about 7 knots. They do not always keep to the starboard-hand side of the river; sometimes they will prefer to swap over to the other side to keep on the inside of a long bend (either to make up for lost time, or keep in the deeper water, as they draw 4m with a full load). If they do maintain a course off the left bank, they warn approaching traffic by displaying a large blue flag protruding from the wheelhouse on the starboard side.

Between Rouen and the Surésnés lock in the suburbs of Paris (a distance by river of 225km), there is mile after mile of delightful countryside. There are several islands in this section, which can cause momentary confusion as to which side they should be passed; the *Seine Guide*, referred to at the end of this chapter, clearly indicates which route should be taken for both up and down traffic. Also shown is the depth of water behind the islands which can serve as a peaceful anchorage, tucked away from the wash of the barges. The meanings of the various traffic signs displayed on the Seine are likewise well illustrated.

The *Guide* shows the position of every kilometre post on the Seine from 355, off Honfleur, to the first post (pk.1) in the centre of Paris, just beyond Notre Dame, off the Ile St Louis. Photographs of both sides of all the Seine bridges are effectively used to show which of the arches should be taken. Although it is a nautical guide, there is interesting information about the various sights to be seen en route. Perhaps the most impressive landmark on the canalised Seine are the ruins of the Château Gaillard, built by Richard the Lion Heart, above Les Andèlys (pk 174). You can climb up to what is left of the Château for marvellous views of the winding Seine below.

The Seine between Rouen and Paris was a great favourite of the French Impressionists; Monet's *Le Pont du Chemin de Fer à Argenteuil* is widely available locally in postcard form. Monét actually had a boat built, which he based at Argenteuil, to paint the banks of the Seine. Just 10 kilometres downstream, Rénoir painted his famous 'Picnic at Bougival'.

Sadly, much of the riverside scenery captured by the Impressionists, no longer exist, having been swallowed up by the growth of Paris's industrial suburbs. The approaches to Paris are disappointing. There seems to be mile upon mile of industry on both sides of the river. The water here is polluted, and a look-out should be kept for timber floating on the oily surface. The passage along this part of the Seine, from the last lock at Suresnes to a first glimpse of the Eiffel Tower, should be covered with a minimum of delays.

For many years, craft visiting Paris had to secure between the Pont Alexandre III and a large barge which belonged to the Touring Club de France. This was magnificently central, almost within a stone's throw of the *Place de la Concorde*. There was, however, one big snag with this quayside mooring; this was the wash of passing craft. In addition to the stream of barges, there are the huge *Bateaux-Mouches* which are out all day and then extend into the evening when they are all lit up, and you can see the passengers enjoying a candle-lit dinner. This may sound all very romantic, but for the visiting yacht crews the wash makes the berths extremely uncomfortable.

The Touring Club de France berths have been improved by the building of wash barriers, but of more significance to boat owners these days is the *Port de Paris Arsenal*. This yacht harbour is 4.5km beyond the Pont Alexandre III and the Touring Club's premises. To port, is the *Jardin des Tuileries* and the *Palais du Louvre*. Having skirted round *Notre-Dame and the Ile St Louis*, there are lock gates to port, leading into the Port de Plaisance which was once the end of the Canal St-Martin. The lock keeper can be contacted on Channel 9. The facilities are excellent – electricity, showers etc. Shops, restaurants, the Metro and the railway station are conveniently close, and it is only a few minutes walk to the *Place de la Bastille*. This is the limit for most yachts, unless continuing along the Seine to connect up with the waterway route through to the Mediterranean.

Note: There is only one guide that covers the Seine between Le Havre and Paris in any great detail. This is No.1 in the *Navicarte* series published in French, English and German by *Editions Cartographiques Maritime*. This highly recommended guide is available in London from Kelvin Hughes or the Stanfords Map Centre.

Somme, Pas-de-Calais, Nord
St-Valéry-sur-Somme – Le Crotoy – Le Hourdel – Le Touquet –
Etaples – Boulogne – Calais – Gravelines – Dunkerque

Cross-Channel Ports: Boulogne, Calais, Dunkerque

Somme

Like most of the Départements in this region of Northern France, the
Somme is trying to attract more visitors. They suffer from having only
20 miles of coastline, which consists of a mere handful of small resorts.
Most of the tourist attractions are several miles inland and would be of
particular interest to visiting yacht crews whose numbers included
twitchers, gardening enthusiasts and lovers of the horse.

The Baie de Somme is 5 miles wide and extends for about 6 miles
inland, from the first channel buoy to the Somme's only deep water
harbour at St Valéry-sur-Somme. Open to North-Westerlies, the sand
banks in the Baie are constantly on the move. There are areas of
quicksand, and the advancing tide comes in at a rate comparable with the
Baie St Michel. Having said that, St Valéry is an excellent yacht harbour
in an interesting town, and attracted around 100 visiting English
yachts in 1991.

It is actually possible to walk from one side of the Baie to the other,
although the local tourist office say that this must only be undertaken
with a qualified guide. Just outside La Mouclade restaurant (highly
recommended) at Le Crotoy, there is a landing pad for a rescue
helicopter, which is called out several times a year to bring in tourists
who have got themselves into difficulties.

Joan of Arc made the walk across the Baie from le Crotoy to St Valéry.
She was a prisoner of the English, and this crossing of the Baie de
Somme was part of a long detour made by her captors to avoid the
French. You can still see the tiny prison where she was held in the old
quarter of St Valéry.

St-Valéry-sur-Somme

The entrance channel to the Baie du Somme is two miles offshore. There
is a visitor's buoy here, where craft can wait in deep water to cross the
offlying sandbanks. This must be attempted on a rising tide and no
earlier than two hours before high water. The channel is certainly well
marked. There are 20 pairs of port and starboard buoys between the

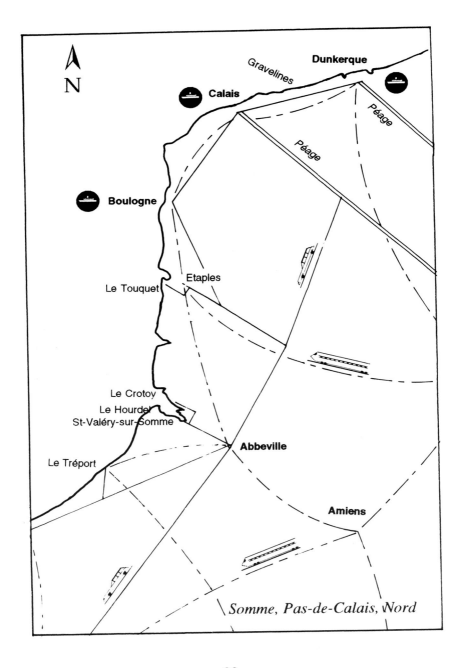

bouée d'attenage and the training wall that extends towards the sea to form the entrance to St Valéry-sur-Somme. This training wall is marked with spar beacons. At No. 20, the channel separates for those craft making for La Hourdel; at No 34, there is another offshoot channel to Le Crotoy. Even with this profusion of marks, care should still be taken to keep in the deep water, so an echo-sounder is a must. Suffice to say that, because of the shifting sands, the buoys just off St Valéry have to be checked daily!

There are deep water pontoon berths at St Valéry, of which 20 are for visitors. The facilities are good, and there is a flourishing yacht club (*Sport Nautique Valéricain*). Access from the road to the pontoons is through a locked gate, and those wishing to enter have to announce themselves to the harbour master. Outside harbour office hours, the gate is worked by using a code obtained when going ashore.

St Valéry-sur-Somme is a small town. One area housed the local fishermen, reflecting the one-time importance of the place as a major fishing port. The town is also divided into the *basse* and *haut* ville. The latter is the old town, with two magnificent gates (Porte Ouest & Porte Est), cobbled streets and fortifications. At St Valéry, the locals claim that this was the port from which William the Conqueror sailed to England. There are actually several harbours that make this claim including Dives-sur-Mer (Calvados). One explanation you might hear (at St Valéry) is that the fleet did set sail from Dives, but were beaten back by the weather and had to reassemble at St Valéry.

Although rarely used by visiting yachts, there is a working lock here which provides access to the Canal de la Somme, linking St Valéry to Abbeville (15kms inland). From there, it is possible to link up with the waterway routes to Belgium, Germany and the Mediterranean.

Le Crotoy

The two other ports in the Somme Département are almost opposite each other, Le Crotoy on East side of the Baie de la Somme and le Hourdel to the West. Le Crotoy is both fishing harbour and Port de Plaisance. However, unlike St Valéry, the pontoon berths have been dredged to a least depth of only one metre. A visit to Le Crotoy should not be made around springs to avoid accidentally being neaped (indeed, this cautionary note applies to the whole of the Baie de Seine). Le Crotoy is also a holiday resort with a fine beach when the tide is right, and with many hotels and a casino. During the season, there is a narrow gauge single track railway linking Le Crotoy, St Valéry and the holiday resort

of Cayeux. The rolling stock is a steam-driven Thomas the Tank-type
engine which pulls three coaches.

Le Hourdel

The last of the three harbours is Le Hourdel. About a dozen fishing boats
are based here, using the quay. There may well be several other fishing
boats from Le Crotoy and St Valéry who prefer to use Le Hourdel to land
their catch because it is nearer to the sea. Small motor boats use the
muddy, drying creek near to the jetty. There are pontoons here, but really
nothing appropriate for visiting yachts.

The Somme's seaside resorts are unspoiled, with beaches almost as far
as you can see at low tide. The most Northerly is Fort-Mahon which
combines with Quend-Plage-les-Pins to provide a long strip of sandy
beach flanked by bathing huts.

Fort-Mahon and Quend-Plage each has its own yacht club, but the
members here mostly sail sand yachts. These are available for hiring, but
because they are capable of an average speed of around 60kph, use of
these craft has to be restricted to a marked out area. The serious sand
yacht speed trials are held a few miles further North at Berck-Plage
which is just in the Pas-de-Calais Département. At Berque Plage, speeds
of over 150kph have been recorded.

Sand yacht

Moving sands around the resorts and harbours, both at sea and on land, are very much a feature of this Somme coastline. There is only one main road in Fort Mahon; this runs at right angles to the sea and yet curiously it is flanked each side by massive sand dunes. The area boasts the largest sand dunes in France.

Between Fort Mahon and Quend-Plage-les-Pins is one of the Somme's new tourist attractions – the Aqua Club *'Côte Picarde'*. This pleasure complex has two swimming pools (one covered and one outside), water toboggans, sauna, Turkish baths, tennis courts, golf, and a restaurant. The modest entrance fee to the site, covers use of every amenity except the *'Cabins de Bronzage'*. With the building of the aqua club it is hoped to create a new community and another holiday resort.

To the South of the Baie de Somme, are Cayeux-sur-Mer, Ault and Mers-les-Bains. Cayeux together with Brighton-les-Bains form a single holiday resort, lined with white painted beach huts in front of which the mile long stretch of high water pebbly beach is covered with planks. Ault is built around the cliffs on several different levels, and boasts of having three beaches. Between the resorts of Ault and Mers-les-Bains are towering white cliffs, said to be the highest in France.

Some would say the most interesting part of the Somme is the *Région Marquentaire* (derived from la *Mer qui est en terre*). Much of the land here was originally covered by the sea – with inland towns such as Abberville and Rue once operating as important sea ports. With advice from experienced Dutch engineers, polders were formed and drained to extend the coastline to seaward by several miles.

In this area is a world-famous ornithological park where some of the rarest birds and plants in Europe can be seen. The site is well laid out, following a 4 km path with guiding notes. There are several hides en route. For children, there is the shorter '*parcours d'initiation*'. The *Parc Ornithologique* is North-West of Le Crotoy. Just South of Le Hourdel is the *Maison de l'Oiseau*, which is a museum of birds displayed most vividly in carefully built, authentic surroundings.

Other popular inshore attractions are the *Abbaye* and *Jardins de Valloires* located on the border, between the Somme and Pas-de-Calais near Argoules. Allow at least an hour and a half to wander round the gardens where there are several thousand different plants. The rose gardens here are famous, but you need to go at the right time of the year to see these roses of Picardy at their best. And for the horse lover? The Henson riding centre near the coast at St-Quentin-en-Tourmont (between Le Crotoy and Quand-Plage) is the home of this local breed of golden horse. The Henson Centre offers rides, competitions, trekking and a tour of the Henson breeding centre.

Pas-de-Calais

Because of its proximity to the coast of England, this Département receives by far and away the most British visitors. Anyone who has stood on the cliffs above Dover is amazed at the amount of ferry traffic in and out. The harbour authorities claim that during the day, a ferry passes through the breakwaters on average every 8 minutes. The effects of the Channel Tunnel on these ferry schedules, remains to be seen over the next few years.

With the shortest crossing (Dover to Calais) a mere 23miles, and only a few miles more from the yacht harbour at Folkestone, it is questionable whether the same principles apply for permanently keeping a boat over the other side. On a clear day, viewed from the high ground around Calais, the white cliffs of Dover, and much more, are clearly visible. So why consider moving the boat from the South coast of England to the Pas-de-Calais coastline?

Certainly the cost argument still applies, with an astonishingly low *tarif* for yachts based in Calais, for instance, where there are full marina facilities including a yacht club. This 'saving' over UK charges more than offsets the cost of several fast Channel-crossings (*SeaCat* takes a mere 35 minutes).

Another consideration is passage-making across the Dover Straits. For smaller boats, this may be a question of having to wait maybe 2 or 3 days for the right weather conditions (particularly good visibility). To a newcomer, this crossing, from the South Coast to France, can be a hair-raising experience, dodging between the streams of traffic and, at the same time, complying with the traffic lane regulations.

Some boat owners will claim that a base on one of the Pas-de-Calais harbours provides little in the way of surrounding places to visit; to many, the mention of Calais and Boulogne conjures up a picture of day-trippers packing the local supermarkets; they then make for the British pub-type bars that are covered in Union Jacks and advertise *'English spoken here'*. There is some truth in this claim, but look a little beyond Calais and Boulogne's tripper image and you will find many attractive features in both towns.

The tourist office for Pas-de-Calais do have a problem. On one hand, they want to encourage the day-trippers to come over to France and spend money. They do not, however, want this image to discourage tourists who might otherwise plan a stay of two or three days in these Channel ports. There are a huge number of visitors who, having been refreshed from a break in the driving during the Channel crossing, immediately make for Brittany or the Mediterranean.

The same situation applies to many a yacht crew – they arrive at Boulogne or Calais and, almost before the lines are secured, the skipper will be looking at the tide-tables to work out the earliest departure time. Conscious of this, facilities for yachts are being closely examined by local *Châmbres de Commerce*, and the attractions of the Pas-de-Calais coastline are being more widely publicised.

To the South of Boulogne are several holiday resorts, built around the long strip of sandy beach that extends almost unbroken for 35km to Berck-Plage. With the exception of Le Touquet, these are very much family resorts amongst the dunes, where, at low water, the beach extends three-quarters of a mile offshore.

Le Touqet

Le Touquet was one of the first holiday resorts of France, catering for wealthy Parisians who were joined by the gentry from England. There is

103

still much evidence of this one-time opulence, with beautiful villas just visible amongst pine trees; there is the fine example of Gothic architecture in the *Hôtel de Ville* and the world-famous *Hôtel Westminster*. The promenade at Le Touquet comes as something of a surprise – it is wide and long, with colourful bathing huts and the beach on one side, but with a tasteful absence on the other side of shops, bars and restaurants. These are to be found in the centre of the town. Unlike the neighbouring resorts, which virtually close up from September to Easter, Le Touquet's smart shops and restaurants in the tree-lined boulevards stay open all the year round.

Le Touquet is situated at the entrance to the drying River Canche. Although the channel is well marked, there is still a possibility of touching in the centre of the channel towards high water neaps. A boat drawing more than 1.2m should avoid entering at high water springs when there might be a danger of getting neaped. Approaching in strong onshore winds is inadvisable.

There are two sailing centres at Le Touquet, the *Base Sud* and the *Base Nord*. The former is on the sea front, and used primarily by day boats and racing dinghies. The *Centre Nautique du Touquet Base Nord* is inside the drying estuary. There is a prominent yacht club here, together with a large workshop. The Club's drying moorings are some way off, close to the entrance channel. A privately funded two-year development plan at the *Base Nord* has already started (1992); this involves building a lock and providing deep water berths for around 700 boats. Access into this new basin will be two hours either side of high water.

Etaples

Further up the Canche River is the fishing port and yacht harbour of Etaples. The emphasis here is very much on the fishing industry; the local fleet cram themselves alongside the quay (to port going up river). There is an interesting fish market here, consisting of a row of white-tiled stalls. On the back of the stalls are glazed tiles showing the names and shapes of all the fish landed here, together with a plan of where each species is likely to be found.

The yacht harbour, beyond the fishing boats, is suitable for small craft only, or those craft that can dry out conveniently alongside pontoons in soft mud. Further progress up river is not possible because of the low road bridge. Boats approaching the pontoons or leaving should allow for a strong tide as the flood can carry a boat uncomfortably close to the

Etaples

bridge. Near to the yacht harbour is the *Capitainerie* and the Tourist Office (who administer the shower block). There are several shops, bars and restaurants nearby, including '*au Pécheurs des Etaples*' with a gastronomic menu that is famous throughout the Region. (Come prepared with a suitable plastic card!)

Boulogne

Although Boulogne (12 miles North of the Canche estuary) is France's most important fishing harbour and second only to Calais in receiving visitors, not much has been done to encourage visiting yachts. There is a small marina (100 berths) in the Avant-Port and another primarily for small motor boats in the Arrière-Port (waiting lists for both). There are just 8 berths for visitors on the outside pontoons in the Avant-Port, but in the height of the season they cram many more in, rafted up alongside each other until they almost meet the fishing fleet that berth across the water on the Quai Gambetta. Yachts cannot berth alongside this Quai unless their owners have the specific permission of the harbour master. It can be difficult to accommodate yachts over 10 metres in length.

The facilities in the Port de Plaisance are sparse, with water and electricity on the quayside. Fuel can be delivered, otherwise it is a walk to the nearest filling station on Boulevard Gambetta.

What the yacht harbours lack in ambience, is certainly made up by the attractions ashore. Old Boulogne, overlooking the docks and dominated by Notre Dame cathedral and the castle, is surrounded by 13th century ramparts which incorporate seventeen towers. It is possible to walk right round the top of the ramparts, and take in the superb view below.

There have been several plans considered for enlarging Boulogne's yachting facilities. Regulations do not allow for any extensions more than 100m from the coastline, so a 'Brighton-type' yacht harbour would not be allowed. One possibility is that with the run-down of the passenger Hovercraft (being replaced by *SeaCats* who use the main port), the Plage de le Portel might be developed, but the *Chambre de Commerce* are looking for a positive sign that there would be a sufficient demand for yacht berths here.

Between Boulogne and Calais (a distance of 23 miles) is Cap Gris-Nez with its lighthouse throwing a beam from one side of the Channel to the other. There is a holiday resort at Wissant with a beach that extends almost all the way to Calais. Up on the high ground near Cap Blanc Nez is Bleriot's monument. This is a good vantage point to gaze across the Channel at the famous White Cliffs on the other side. Also located along this stretch of coastline is the start of the Eurotunnel at Sangatte. In 1992 the evidence of this was limited to vast machinery parked behind wire fencing. There is, however, a permanent exhibition of the project open to the public at Sangatte.

Calais

Compared with Boulogne, Calais has excellent facilities for yachts, providing you do not mind the overcrowding. The yacht harbour is in the Bassin de l'Ouest which has three openings (both lock and road bridge) around high water. Outside the basin, there are moorings which can be used if waiting for an opening. Inside the basin, there are 134 individual pontoons, with 90 metres of pontoon-space for visitors. During the season it is sometimes very nearly possible to walk from one side of the basin to the other, across the decks of visiting yachts.

There are showers at the Société des Régates de Calais whose clubhouse overlooks the basin. Not surprisingly, there is a waiting list for permanent berths in the Bassin de l'Ouest; curiously, if a yacht makes constant use of the Port de Plaisance as a visitor on the daily rate, when the cumulative sum paid reaches the annual *tarif*, the rest of the stay during any one year is free.

Calais

It is possible to join the inland waterway system at Calais by entering the lock to gain access to the Bassin Carnot. The yacht club staff will drop a visiting yacht's mast for a nominal charge. Once in the waterway network, a yacht can reach the Mediterranean via Paris or the Marne.

Like Boulogne, Calais is trying to attract visitors other than those whose stay in the town is mostly spent in one of several hypermarkets, or those who arrive on a car ferry and drive through the town without stopping (this is even more likely since the opening of the A16 linking Calais direct to the motorway system).

There are three conspicuous landmarks in the town – the unmistakable *Hôtel de Ville*, curiously built around 1920 in an ornate, colourful neo-Flemish style; in front of the town hall is Rodin's famous bronze statue 'Burghers of Calais'. Any school child should be able to tell you about these six leading citizens of the town; Edward III had invaded France, and captured Calais after an eight-month siege. The custom at that time was for all the town's people to be killed by the occupying troops for resisting for so long. These six worthy citizens offered their lives to Edward III in return for sparing the rest of the inhabitants. He agreed with this arrangement, and then spared the lives of the six as a result of his wife pleading their case. The English stayed on here for another 200 years.

The other two landmarks are old lighthouses. The 13th-century Watch Tower, in the Place d'Armes, was used as a lighthouse until 1849; the other, until recent years, served the harbour. This one is located to the East of the yacht harbour and can now be climbed for a spectacular view over the town and out to sea.

Much of Calais was flattened during the two World Wars. Some of the old buildings that escaped are the *Citadel* (now converted into a Sports Stadium), two forts and Notre Dame Church which is remarkable because some of it was built around 1400 by the occupying English – hence the uniquely English-style architecture. There are two museums – one featuring fine arts and lace; the other, in a German blockhaus, is devoted to World War II. Calais also has a good bathing beach within a few minutes walk from the yacht harbour.

Nord

It would be a mistake to gloss over the Nord Département coastline between Calais and the Belgian border, simply because much of it is highly industrialised. There are, in this 28 miles of coastline, two small holiday resorts and two harbours. It remains, however, somewhat inhospitable with limited resources for visiting yachts, and with sand banks extending several miles offshore.

Gravelines

The two Nord ports – Gravelines and Dunkerque – are perhaps worth keeping an eye on for the future. Gravelines was one of 13 towns fortified by Vauban. The best view of the fortifications is from the air, because the preserved walls and moat are built round the town to form a perfect star.

Gravelines is another of those towns which was originally a major fishing port, but, over the centuries, the moving sands have left the town 500 metres inland. It is now reached via the River Aa (popular with compilers of French crosswords). To the North of Gravelines, where once it was sea, polders have been formed and drained. The communities of Grande-Fort-Philippe and Petite-Fort-Philippe have been built up on the reclaimed land, either side of the River Aa. On one of these polders, at Petit-Fort-Philippe, is 'Espace International', the largest Sports and Cultural Centre in the North of France.

As things stand at the moment (1992), Gravelines does not have much to offer visiting yachts. There are sand banks almost right across the entrance which is completely exposed to the North/North-East. At low water springs, hardly anything remains afloat in the River Aa, although the huge numbered port and starboard marks might make you think to the contrary. There is a dinghy sailing club to port on entering and then two tiny drying harbours used by small local motor boats. The yacht harbour for visitors is in the Bassin Vauban, just upriver of the town. This is not, however, used as a *bassin-à-flot*; there is a lock gate which could be worked, but the local boat owners prefer it to remain open between 15 June and 15 September, so that they have more freedom to enter and leave the river (although a bridge opening is still necessary).

There are improvements underway at Gravelines – the first part of the building project is to prevent further silting up by extending both piers in the entrance to the river. The second phase is to dredge the river to provide access to deep water berths four hours either side of high water. Gravelines is another possible entry via the Aa to France and Belgium's inland waterways.

Much of the original fortifications at Gravelines survived World War II, despite a 4-day battle between French Units and German Panzer Divisions; this effectively drew the German Army away from Dunkerque and allowed the evacuation of the English army from the beaches.

Dunkerque

Dunkerque will, for many more years, be associated with the mass evacuation of more than 300,000 troops. This was undertaken by vessels of all sizes, including the famous armada of Little Ships. They were used for ferrying troops from the beaches between Malo-les-Bains and Bray-Dunes to the larger ships waiting offshore. To-day, Malo-les-Bains and

Bray-Dunes are modest holiday resorts – the last before the Belgian frontier.

Dunkerque to-day has few reminders of the last war – unless you include the blocks of uniformly grey buildings. Eighty per cent of the town and docks were completely wiped out. In the reconstruction of the town, priority was given to the docks and industry; the port is now the third largest in France. There are facilities for yachts in the docks, but Dunkerque has never been able to attract many visiting yachts. Boat owners who do call here will find a pontoon berth in the 'Avant Port' or in one of the old dock basins. There are actually several yacht clubs close to the pontoons, and the facilities are reasonable. Those who do plan to attract more visiting craft, do have something of a problem. Most passage-making yachts, along this stretch of French coastline, are either making for or returning from the Belgian ports or Vlissingen (Flushing) where the Dutch waterways from one side of Holland to the other start/finish.

Dunkerque's Chamber of Commerce know that there are over 10,000 pleasure craft with the DK registration, and for this fleet there are a paltry 600 places. Some of the local boats have moved on up the coast to Nieuport, which is an excellent yacht harbour. Another problem with Dunkerque is that the sailing resources are spread about the port in four separate places, each with their own clubhouse. They seem to work well together – for example if there is a gale from the North-West when the Avant Port can get uncomfortable, yachts left unattended may well be moved from an exposed pontoon into the inner basin.

Undeterred, work has already started (1992) on the first phase of an ambitious development plan. This first phase is to create a new 400 berth marina, with a *Capitainerie* and Clubhouse. This is to port on entering in a disused shipyard, just beyond the entrance to the canal. The next phase is to build a new lock (to starboard on entering, opposite the new marina). This will provide access to several basins and will make provision for many more pontoon berths in the Bassin de Commerce. It is also planned to amalgamate all the yacht clubs by providing a grand new clubhouse. Like neighbouring Gravelines, Dunkerque is another port providing access to the inland waterways.

So, what of the future for Dunkerque? Undoubtedly it will soon become an important yachting centre, offering berths for a reasonable *tarif*. It is a good base for anyone who wants to cruise further Eastwards, to Belgium and Holland and beyond. The Sally Line has regular sailings between Ramsgate and West Dunkerque (14km from the ferry terminal to the town centre, so bus or taxi required.) Dunkerque is yet one more example of local enterprise improving yachting facilities – well worth keeping an eye on the progress of this major development.

Bray Dunes

4 Travel to France

Eurotunnel

Not all that many years ago, boring a tunnel beneath the Dover Straits that would link France with England, was little more than a futuristic dream, along with landing men on the moon. And here we are, within months of being able transport our cars on the railway between Folkestone and Calais.

Some boat owners must be wondering whether it still makes sense to spend a miserable 24 hours struggling against the elements to cross from the Solent to, say, Cherbourg. The worry, the cold, the sea sickness, and the thought of having to make the return journey – is it all a bit pointless? Would some of the crew prefer to use the Channel Tunnel or take a cross-channel ferry?

In many ways, the existence of the Channel Tunnel and the increased competition between the ferry operators, adds strength to the argument for basing the yacht on the French side of the Channel.

The Channel Tunnel sounds almost too good to be true. In the late summer of 1993, we will be able to turn up in the car without having booked, and drive almost straight on to the Eurotunnel shuttle. Eurotunnel claim that with 4 shuttles an hour at peak periods, there will be the minimum of queuing, even at holiday times.

Eurotunnel believe they have one big advantage over the ferry operators – they can guarantee the service 24 hours a day for 365 days in the year uneffected by heavy seas. For Eurotunnel customers there is no listening to shipping forecasts or that last minute rush to the chemist for sea-sick pills. And the time taken to cross is just 35 minutes, platform to platform (27 minutes in the tunnel).

As the motorists approach Folkestone, they can tune in to Eurotunnel Radio to find out the time of the next shuttle departure plus information on the weather and traffic conditions on the other side. At the entrance to the terminal, the motorist simply pulls up to the toll-booth and hands over money or a credit card to pay for the crossing. Having driven on to the shuttle, this will be moved through the tunnel by electric locomotives, capable of speeds of up to 80mph. Driver and passengers can, if they wish, cross to France without ever leaving their car. Others may prefer to walk along the shuttle to join other passengers watching the indicator boards flash by as the shuttle hurtles towards France.

The Channel Tunnel will not be available for foot passengers (anyone who is not in a car, coach or lorry will be on one of the 31 high-speed trains travelling daily between London and Paris/Brussels). British Rail /SNCF are not permitted to sell duty-frees. Car drivers and passengers will, almost certainly, have the opportunity of buying duty-frees at the Eurotunnel terminal at Folkestone.

Cross-channel ferry routes

Company	Route	Sailings (24Hrs)		Duration (Hrs)	
		High	Low	Day	Night
Brittany	Plymouth-Roscoff	3	1	6	8
Ferries	Porstsmouth-St Malo	2	1	9	11
	Portsmouth-Caen	3	2	6	7*
Truckline	Poole-Cherbourg	2	1		
Hoverspeed	Folkestone-Boulogne	6	3	¾	1
	Dover-Boulogne	5	3	¾	
	Dover-Calais (SeaCat)	10	5	¾	
	" " (Hovercraft)	12	8	½	
P & O	Portsmouth-Cherbourg	4	1	4¾	7
European	Portsmouth-Le Havre	3	3	5¾	7
	Dover-Boulogne	6	6	1¾	
	Dover-Calais	20	14	1¼	
Sealink	S'hampton-Cherbourg	2	1		
Stena	Newhaven-Dieppe	4	2	4	
	Dover-Calais	18	12		
Sally Line	Ramsgate-Dunkerque	5	5	2½	

*Varies depending on tides

Brittany Ferries' Flagship *'MV Normandie'*

P&O European Ferries Superferry *'Pride of Dover'*

Hoverspeed *Great Britain*

Stena Sealinks *'Stena Normandy'*

Brittany Ferries

The story of the formation of Brittany Ferries by Alexis Gourvennec is a fascinating one. He was a Breton farmer and also the leader of one of the largest agricultural co-operatives in Brittany. Prior to 1973, the only way to transport their produce to the UK was via Paris.

Four thousand farmers from the region decided to set up their own shipping company and build a deep-water harbour at Roscoff. In January 1973, a converted tank landing craft became a regular freight service between Roscoff and Plymouth. There were, at that time, no passenger services between Brittany and the UK (British Railways having found the Southampton – St Malo route uneconomical a good many years earlier). With the freight service, came the demand for a scheduled passenger service between Roscoff and Plymouth, and a custom-built passenger Ro-Ro was commissioned which came into service in 1974.

From these humble origins, Brittany Ferries is now the major ferry operator on the Western Channel. The company acquired *Truckline*, a freight service operating between Poole and Cherbourg, which was expanded to include cars and passengers. 1992 saw the introduction of a superferry – the 27,000 ton *Normandie*, which is Brittany Ferries' new flagship, operating between Portsmouth and Caen. She can carry 2,120 passengers, 420 cars and 40 freight vehicles. Another new ferry, again launched in 1992, is the 20,500 ton *Barfleur* operating a year-round passenger service between Poole and Cherbourg. *Barfleur* can carry 1,200 passengers and 600 cars or 118 freight vehicles.

In the context of this book, Brittany Ferries is the sole operator between the UK and Calvados (Caen), Ile-et-Vilaine (St Malo), and Finistère (Roscoff); Brittany Ferries is also one of several operators using Cherbourg, the only ferry port in the Manche Département.

Brittany Ferries operate a 'French Property Owners Club' whose UK members own property in France (not yet extended to boat owners who base their craft in France). There is an enrolment fee and an annual subscription. By travelling outside peak-time sailings, discounts of up to 30% are available on standard passenger and vehicle fares, plus a 10% discount in the ferry restaurants. There is also the '*Matelots Club*' for children (4–13) who, in addition to receiving various promotional kits, also qualify for a visit to the bridge with every third crossing they take.

Passengers on night crossings will only be allowed on board without a cabin or reclining seat if all such accommodation has been allocated.

Hoverspeed

In June 1990, Hoverspeed's latest addition to their fleet, achieved what was, by any standards, a PR man's dream. The world's largest and most advanced catamaran. *Hoverspeed Great Britain* crossed the Atlantic in 3 days, 7 hours and 52 minutes. This 'Blue Riband' crossing gained, after some legal haggling, the Hales Trophy for the fastest crossing of the Atlantic by a passenger ship. She then went on to win the 'Blue Riband' of the Channel.

The original design of the *SeaCat* was pioneered by Hoverspeed's parent company 'Sea Containers' to be gradually phased in to replace the five Hovercraft operating on the English Channel.

The first SeaCat *Hoverspeed Great Britain* was initially deployed on the Portsmouth/Cherbourg route, where it encountered some minor teething troubles.

In 1991, *Hoverspeed Great Britain* was redeployed in Dover working alongside the third SeaCat in the series, *Hoverspeed France* providing services from Dover to Calais and Boulogne.

The fourth craft in the first phase of building was delivered in March 1992 to expand the Channel network even further with the introduction of a Folkestone / Boulogne route in April.

Hoverspeed claim that the design problems with the SeaCat have been resolved and theses giant catamarans now function with a minimum of passenger discomfort in wave heights up to 3.5 metres.

One cannot fail to be impressed by the SeaCats. Five storeys high and capable of taking 450 passengers and 80 cars, these ships are designed to cruise at 44 knots crossing the Channel in 35 minutes to Calais and 45 minutes to Boulogne. Passengers can stroll around the decks, visit the snack bar or duty free shop.

Those travelling regularly with Hoverspeed can enrol as members of the Blue Riband Club and renew their membership at the end of twelve months if they have made three or more return trips over that period. Benefits of membership include a direct line into the reservation system, a priority waiting list for unreserved bookings and a complimentary drink on board. Members also get their own allocated seating and steward service.

P&O European Ferries

P&O European Ferries operate two superferries – *Pride of Dover* and *Pride of Calais* – on the 75 minute crossing between Dover and Calais. These 26,000 ton vessels can each take up to 650 cars and 2,290 passengers. Without having to make provision for accommodation for night crossings, these Superferries have plenty of space for restaurants, cafeterias and lounges. A third Superferry, the stretched and refurbished *Pride of Kent* re-joined the P&O cross-channel fleet in 1992.

A feature on all the P&O cross-channel routes is the *Club Class* style of travelling. By paying a small supplement, P&O travellers can make exclusive use of the *Club Class* lounge on all the P&O fleet. On the shorter crossings, this space is furnished with tables and lounge seats. Free coffee/tea is available with a choice of newspapers. The *Club Class* accommodation on the Cherbourg and Le Havre routes consists of rows of comfortable reclining seats, which are more than adequate for a night crossing if no cabin space is available. For those who cannot be parted from their business affairs, telephone and fax is available to *Club Class* passengers.

P&O European Ferries is the only operator to offer discounts to shareholders. Passengers must be registered holders on the 31st December, of the required nominal amount of P&O 5.5% Redeemable Non Cumulative Stock. This Concessionary Stock must be registered by the 31st December to qualify for discounts in the following year (note: registry can take several weeks). 300-599 shares qualify the owner to a half discount; 600 of shares entitle the owner to a full discount. On the Portsmouth-Cherbourg and Portsmouth – Le Havre routes, the full discount is 40%; on the Dover-Boulogne and Dover-Calais routes ,there is a 50% discount. The named shareholder must make the booking which must include a car, but the discount applies to the shareholder + up to 3 passengers + car. The concession cannot be extended to cover overnight accommodation or the restaurants.

Full details from P&O European Ferries, Concessionary Fare Department, Channel House, Channel View Road, Dover, Kent CT17 9TJ.

Another scheme operated by P&O European Ferries is *'Motor Points'*. A fully paid return fare including car (on any of the P&O European routes) scores 10 points; a single fare with car or 60-hour/120-hour return trips scores 5 points.10 points earns a 20% discount off the next crossing with P&0 European. For an accumulated 30 points, the traveller can choose from a wide range of selected gifts. 45 points earns a free return ticket for car and four adults. The points must fall within a 12 months period to qualify, and passages on which bonus discounts or share discounts have already been claimed do not qualify. This scheme is popular with UK owners of property in France as it will also be to boat owners who have based their boats across the Channel. (Further details from Channel House.)

Sealink Stena

Stena, the Swedish operator, bought Sealink in 1990. Since then, much has been done to streamline the fleet to operate more effectively on the money earning routes. The Folkestone – Boulogne service closed at the end of 1991; in the same year Sealink Stena introduced a new service between Cherbourg and Southampton, provided by the refurbished *Stena Normandy* which is the largest ferry on the Western side of the Channel.

On the Dover-Calais service, four ships are in service all year round. Two are British (*Stena Fantasia* and *Stena Invicta*) and two French (*Fiesta* and *Côte d'Azur*). *Stena Fantasia* and sister ship *Fiesta* are each 25,000 tons with capacities for 710 cars and 1,800 passengers.

Sealink Stena try to achieve a fun cruise-line atmosphere on their ships. The amazing domes on the decks of the Stena Fantasia and Fiesta are not some nuclear early-warning radar device; they house video games, vending machines and discos, popular even on these short hauls. *Stena Normandy*, plying between Southampton and Cherbourg has a casino, night club, cinema, a children's entertainments officer and live cabaret.

Passengers on the night sailing from Southampton must have reserved accommodation (either a cabin or a reclining seat).

Sealink Stenna offer special terms to boat owners who now base their craft on the French side of the Channel. To qualify for a 20% discount, the boat owner must book through the Dover or Southampton travel centres where papers must be produced to establish that their boat is genuinely based in France. The 20% discount, off the standard single or return foot passenger fare, applies to boat owners and crew. This discount is available on the Southampton/Cherbourg and Dover/Calais services.

Sally Ferries

Started in 1982, Sally is the baby amongst the giants. The line has just two ships, *Sally Star* and *Sally Sky*, operating exclusively between Ramsgate and Dunkerque. They maintain a schedule of 5 sailings from Ramsgate over a 24 hour period, every day and night of the year except for Christmas Day, with reduced sailings on Christmas Eve and Boxing Day.

Sally Line has equipped its ships to attract families. Children under 14 go free when travelling by car. The on-board facilities include a supervised crèche for 2–8 year olds, mother and baby facilities and play rooms. For the parents, each ship has a bar, casino, cafeteria and Smorgasbord restaurant. *Sally Sky* has a fast food brasserie; *Sally Star* has a Juke Box Video Café and a fruit machine arcade. Both ships have a tax-free *Benetton* shop.

Sally Line also appeals to those motorists wanting to avoid traffic queues at both departure and arrival ports (there is rarely any congestion around the terminals at both Ramsgate and Dunkerque).

The Dunkerque terminal is actually 8 miles from the town centre (and the yacht harbour), but for foot passengers Sally Line operates coaches that meet the 0900 and 1100 outward sailings, taking foot passengers from the ferry terminal to the town centre (and the hypermarché). The reverse coach trips leave the town to catch the 1700 and 2030 return sailings.

Sally Line also operates the *Discovery Club*. For an annual subscription, members receive a card which is stamped every time they make use of the Sally line. The cumulative stamps entitle members to discounted passages or free day trips.

By air

① AIGLE AZUR Gatwick – Deauville
① AIR FRANCE Heathrow – Nantes
① AIR VENDREE Gatwick – Rouen
② AURIGNY AIR SERVICES Jersey/Guernsey – Cherbourg, Dinard
① BRIT AIR Gatwick – Brest, Caen, Le Havre, Quimper, Rennes
③ LOVEAIR Lydd – Le Touquet
④ JERSEY EUROPEAN AIRWAYS Jersey – Dinard

① c/o *Air France*, Colet Court, 100 Hammersmith Road, London
W67JP   Reservations 081 742 6600
② *Aurigny Air Services*, Ayline House, States Airport, Alderney
Channel Islands.   Reservations 0481 822886
③ *Loveair*, Lydd Ashford Airport, Lydd, Kent
Reservations 0679 21416
④ *Jersey European Airways*, Jersey Airport, St Peter, Jersey
Reservations 0534 45661

Travel in France

Use of a car in France is obviously not a priority if the boat has a permanent berth at one of the following cross-channel terminals – St Malo, Cherbourg, Le Havre or the Picardy ports. There is a waiting list for permanent berths at both Caen and Ouistreham (Brittany Ferries terminal) and likewise at Morlaix (nearest yacht basin to Brittany Ferries Roscoff terminal).

If travelling by ferry to Ouistreham or Roscoff, it may well still be possible to reach the boat using public transport. The alternative base to Ouistreham might, for example, be the yacht harbour at Dives (Port Guillaume) where there are plenty of vacancies. Dives is only 20km from Caen, and there are bus and train services between the two.(A ferry bus runs between Caen and Ouistreham to meet up with the arrivals/departures). The author has suggested Brest as a possible home port for a boat owner who prefers to use the Plymouth – Roscoff ferry. Again, it is relatively easy to get from Roscoff to Brest by public transport; there are several ways of getting from Roscoff to Morlaix (train or bus); it is then just 32 minutes by fast train (54 by slow, stopping) from Morlaix to Brest.

If the boat owner chooses a base in the Vilaine River, for example, on the West coast, or Ploumanach on the North coast, then a car is essential, and the ferry cost of taking a car over to France must be taken into consideration. Alternatively, do not take out a car; hire one instead from a mainline railway station. Even if the boat owner has a permanent base for the yacht conveniently near to one of the ferry terminals, there are obvious advantages in having a car available – if the weather looks set foul, the crew can then travel inland to seek some alternative entertainment.

Rail (SNCF)

Listed below are routes which have stations in coastal towns between Dunkerque and St Nazaire.

(Amiens) – Etaples-Le Touquet- Boulogne – Calais
Calais – Dunkerque
(Paris) – Le Tréport
Rouen – Dieppe
Dives/Cabourg – Trouville/Deauville
Cherbourg – Carentan – Caen

Caen – (Dol)
(Dol)- Dinard – St Malo
(Dol) – St Brieuc – (Guingamp)
(Guincamp) – Paimpol
(Guincamp) – Lannion
(Dol) – (Rennes)
(Rennes) – St Brieuc – Morlaix – Brest
(Rennes) – Redon – Vannes – Auray – Lorient – Quimper
Quimper – Douarnenez
Quimper – Camaret
Quimper – Brest
Redon – St Nazaire
Nantes – St Nazaire – Le Croisic
Nantes – Pornic
Places in brackets are inland, and may be the place to change trains.

An example of travelling by train from St Malo to Vannes:
The 2100 night ferry from Portsmouth to St Malo is scheduled to arrive at 0815. Train leaves St Malo at 0930 and arrives Rennes 10.32. Change. Train leaves Rennes at 10.43 and arrives Vannes 1154.

Vannes is an excellent place to change crews (unfortunately, there is a waiting list for permanent berths here). The author has made this trip several times. It can be a bit of a scramble at St Malo, and you often see other yachting folk standing at the head of the queue of foot passengers waiting to disembark so that they can nab the first taxi to the railway station. When booking the outward journey from Portsmouth, check with Brittany Ferries that the sailing will be on time arriving at St Malo – the night crossing can take longer than usual because of the tide.

French trains are efficiently run and cost significantly less per kilometre compared with British Rail.

Shops and Services

Shopping in France can be a positive pleasure, and, with one or two exceptions, there is a price incentive to take the absolute minimum of stores from the UK.

Best value in France: table wine, beer (packs of Alsace bottled), cheese, champagne, ground coffee, mineral water, fish, packet soups, bars of chocolate (sold for cooking, consumed as eating)

Expensive (*compared with UK prices*): packets of tea biscuits, breakfast cereals, instant coffee, tea bags, fruit juice.

The French pride themselves in the quality of their tins of fruit, vegetables and meats, and the choice is as comprehensive as in the U.K.

Supermarchés/Hypermarchés

Opening hours -

Supermarchés: Tuesday to Saturday 8 a.m.- 8 p.m., some closing for lunch 12.30 – 2.

Hypermarchés: Tuesday to Saturday 8 a.m. to 8 p.m. (some open until 10 p.m.). Monday afternoons (when food shops are closed).

Food in France is distributed with great efficiency and maximum competition, particularly between the hypermarkets. There will be at least one of these in or around most of the larger towns. The nationwide chains include *Auchan, Carrefour, Euromarché, Intermarché, Leclerc* and *Mammouth.* Whether a supermarché can advertise itself as a hypermarché depends on the amount of space exclusively devoted to selling. Many of them really are vast, and will sell everything from a needle and thread to a car wing mirror. They have huge car parks with a garage selling cut-price fuel. Some will have a crèche and maybe a large cafeteria where shoppers can have an amazingly cheap three-course lunch. The weekly shopping can be the family day-out. Many of the supermarchés are situated on the outskirts of the town and will, therefore, be of limited value for stocking up the ship's stores. It defeats the object of the exercise if a taxi has to be taken to and from the supermarché. Much better to take advantage of being in a port when the market is in town. Some boat owners carry a fold-up trolley on board for bulk shopping.

Markets

Opening hours:
Varies considerably from region to region. Weekdays mostly 8 a.m. to 12 noon. Saturdays 8 a.m. to 4 p.m.

There is a list of market days by Département on page. 130. This is not exhaustive, omitting those markets in the larger coastal towns where there could be several, including some covered that operate daily (except for Sundays and Mondays). Fish markets at the main fishing ports may be for wholesalers only, but there will always be an impromptu stall set up on the town quay as the fishing boats unload.

Much of the food on display at the local market will be more expensive than your out-of-town hypermarché, but who's complaining when much of the produce displayed will have been gathered the day before or even that morning.

Shops

Opening hours:
8 a.m. to 12 noon and then 2.30 p.m. or 3 to 7 p.m. or 8 (Tuesday to Saturday).

Food shops may also open for a few hours on Sunday mornings and public holidays. If there are several *boulangeries* in the town, one of them may open on Sunday morning and Monday morning. If there is only one boulangerie for several miles, this may well have to open seven days a week, but just for an hour or two on Sunday and Monday mornings.

Food shops

Baker (boulangerie)

The boulangerie is one of the great institutions of France. Someone in the boat owner's crew should be nominated to nip ashore first thing for the croissants and a *ficelle* or flute (these are the thin sticks of bread which at that time will still be warm). Break off chunks of the bread, add butter, jam, the *croissants* and a cup of steaming coffee, and you have your perfect breakfast. An alternative to the croissant on display at the boulangerie is the brioche – a rich bun, yellow inside; or the *pain au chocolat* – puff pastry with chocolate in the middle.

The next size up in the French loaves is the baguette. This is admirably shaped for cutting into large slices, filling with a salad and then consumed with a bottle of red wine as part of a picnic lunch, either on the beach or on board. The largest French loaf is simply called a *pain*, but unless you are feeding a large crew, buy the *baguette* to be consumed the same day, for French bread does not keep. The *boule* is a large round loaf, sometimes with its own regional taste, like the *Boule Dieppoise*. The *pain de campagne* is a flavoured granary loaf. *Pain de Mie* (sliced/tranche) is about the only loaf suitable for toasting (a rare practice in France) or for making up English-type sandwiches.

By law, every town and village over a certain size has to have a *boulangerie* or *'un depot de pain'*. The owners of boulangeries work long hours, opening at 8 a.m., having already been up for some time to produce the first of the day's batch (they usually bake twice daily). In small villages where there may only be a *bar/tabac*, this acts as the *'depot de pain'*, taking delivery once a day from the nearest boulangerie.

Butcher (boucherie)

There is still some suspicion among British visitors about what they are offered by the butcher. This prejudice may be because some boucheries sell horsemeat, quite legitimately, advertising this service to many consumers who actually prefer horsemeat to beef or veal. The boucherie will go to some lengths to prepare the meat to each customer's requirements. This shop is perhaps of less importance to your average boat owner, whose craft is not equipped to produce a Sunday roast. What about steaks for cooking under the grill? Take time to explain what you want – if you simply ask for bifteck, the crew may be disappointed because the choice of meat was left to the boucherie; likewise, if you ask for bifteck hache, you may be offered mince that has been compressed and can only be served up as hamburgers.

Cake shop (pâtisserie)

Sometimes combined with a boulangerie. Everything is homemade, ranging from exotic strawberry cakes to éclairs. Expensive compared with UK. Shop here for a delicious dessert.

Confectioner (Confiserie)

These are up-market shops (with prices to match), selling hand-made chocolates and sweets, often beautifully packed in minute boxes, held together with ribbon. Also sell boxed collections of small jars of jam. All expensive, but can provide a classy present to take back to the U.K.

Delicatessen (charcuterie)

In many respects, for on-board catering, the charcuterie is a better bet than the boucherie. It is here that you can view a number of pâtés (another great filler for the picnic lunch). Ham, here, is sliced to your directions, and makes an excellent main dish. The charcuterie is also a pork butcher, serving uncooked pork and streaky bacon (often cut very thickly). Various sausages will be on display, but again children in the crew may be suspicious of the contents, and prefer something from the supermarket. In the window will be a mouth-watering selection of salads, which are scooped into small containers and sealed with a lid – again useful for taking back to the boat, but pricey.

Fishmonger (poissonnerie)
Usually found in the larger towns, the poissonnerie is a fascinating display of the many varieties of fish. The squeamish may be put off buying something that is still very much alive before cooking.The poissonnier will take great pride in the shop display of shellfish which, in some places in Normandy and Brittany, will have been cultivated locally. Some will painstakingly fill an old dinghy or a wheelbarrow and park it on the pavement outside.

Grocer (épicerie/alimentation générale)
Thankfully, the small local grocer has not been forced out of business by the supermarchés and hypermarchés. True, some have been turned into self-service, but there is still a welcome when you enter the shop and an 'Au Revoir, m'sieurdame' as you leave. They work long hours and they keep to reasonable prices. If the boat is near, a useful place to buy either cartons of small bottles of beer or large bottles sold singly. They will give a small refund on wine bottles, which can be the easiest way of disposing of them. You can virtually stock up with all basic provisions at the épicerie, and get daily milk here. (The crémerie seems to be something from the past, rarely found in the centre of towns or villages). Milk from the épicerie is sold in four varieties – *lait entier* (full-cream), *demi-écréme* (semi-skimmed), *écréme* (skimmed) and UHT long-life. Unless you have cold storage on board, *lait entier* will go off very quickly, and it is better to compromise with *demi-écréme*.

Other Shops and Services
Bookshop (libraire) A large bookshop in a coastal town may also act as the local agent for French Admiralty charts. Many bookshops will also sell stationery *(papeterie)*, magazines and newspapers (possibly one or two English). The latter display the sign *'journaux'*.

Chemist (Pharmacie) Recognised by large green cross (illuminated when open) outside shop. If closed, there will be a notice indicating the 'duty chemist'. The *pharmacien* is highly qualified, and may suggest treatment that avoids finding the local doctor. Some drugs can be purchased without a prescription (see Medical care on p138.). The *pharmacie* usually stocks medical items only, although some may also have beauty treatments and perfume. There is no shop equivalent to Boots the Chemist.

Hardware store (droguerie, and not to be confused with pharmacie) Essentially a pots and pans shop also selling glassware, buckets, bowls, binliners, cutlery and much more besides. The *droguerie* may stock *camping gaz* and often replacement cylinders of butane (can be difficult if trying to trade in an English non-standard cylinder).

Ironmonger (quincaillerie) Apart from the hypermarché, this is the only shop where you can buy tools, nails, nuts, bolts, etc. May be essential to find one to buy materials to carry out emergency repairs.

Tobacconist (tabac) These have the red carotte sign outside. There can be many variations of what goes on inside. Some will also be bars, stock newspapers and magazines, postcards and stamps, and, in a small village, may also be the local *'dépôt au pain'*. This shop may be the only place to get your *'télécarte'* for the public 'phone, and may be a bus stop where you are obliged to buy your bus ticket.

Banks (banques) In towns, the banks usually open Monday to Friday 0900 – 1200 and 1400 to 1600. Closed Saturday/Sunday or Sunday /Monday. You might be in a large marina where the local shops and services are those more usually found in a small village. In this situation, the local bank may only open up for a couple of mornings a week (and this only in the season). It may be necessary to fund an unforeseen drama (like having the boat's engine stripped down). This can be done quickly, even at a small bank who will contact their regional headquarters who in turn will fax or telex your bank to get authority to release the funds required.The *Eurocheque* is a useful way of paying bills in France or withdrawing money. Most credit cards are now widely accepted. If the boat has a permanent berth in France, it may make sense to open an account locally, and have the advantage of being able to use cash dispensers.

Post office (bureau de poste – PTT) Hours (main post office) 0800 – 1900 Monday to Friday, closing midday for a couple of hours. 0800 – 1200 on Saturdays.There are the inevitable queues. Make sure you are in the right one, and not in a desperately slow-moving queue dealing with business mail, registering, franking mounds of parcels etc.It is a waste of time queuing up for stamps *(timbres)*, if these are just for postcards or letters. These can be bought almost anywhere that sells postcards. When asking for stamps, there is no need to indicate that the postcard is destined for Angleterre, as the postal rate is the same whether it is internal mail or overseas to another country in the EEC. Post boxes (bright yellow) in country districts may have only one collection in the day, and this may be in the middle of the morning.

Receiving mail in France from the UK can be tricky for boat crews. In theory you can ask someone in the UK to address mail *'poste restante'* c/o the local main post office. This can mean queuing and then identifying yourself with a passport and paying a nominal fee. Or you queue only to be told there is nothing for you. That missive you were waiting for, can then, on your instructions, be redirected by the post office to another main post office, perhaps following the boat owner on a cruise all round Brittany. Much better to get your mail sent to a yacht club or harbour office. If you want something from the UK within 24 hours (such as an impeller for example) get your UK stockist to send it out by an international courier service who are extremely efficient and well worth the expense.

Telephones Not all that long ago, public telephones were only available at post offices. You would stand in the queue and pass on the number to someone on the other side of the counter. You then hung around for a few minutes until a bell rang and you were urgently directed to a cubicle. After the phone call, you would again hang around until the telephone exchange had worked out the cost of the call and passed this back to the post office. If not in a hurry, it was a time for exchanging pleasantries with the locals.

Now it is all automatic dialling, dropping 50c, 1f, 5f and 10f pieces into slots or using a 'phone card' *(télécarte)*. More and more public telephones have been converted to *télécarte* only, and it is wise to have one or two on board just in case. They can be purchased at post offices, some tabacs and some cafés. The phone box should have a notice listing the nearest suppliers. Restaurants often have a public phone for the convenience of diners, but invariably these will take 1f pieces only.

From France to UK, dial 19 (wait for change of tone) then 44 followed by UK std code (less the first zero) and then the number. Cheap rates (50% extra time) are weekdays between 10.30 pm and 8 am, weekends after 2 pm on Saturdays. These are local times, so cheap calls from France operate from 9. 30 pm UK time which can be useful.

Directory Enquiries 12 (small charge)
Operator 13
Ambulance 15
Police 17
Fire 18

Electricity 220 volt electricity supply on marina pontoons. Needs a two-pin plug adaptor (widely available in UK).

Coastal markets

(By Département and excludes some of the larger coastal towns, where there may be several markets and some which operate daily)

Manche
Monday: Carentan
Tuesday: Barfleur, Port-Bail, Cherbourg
Wednesday: Granville
Thursday: Cherbourg
Friday: Nil
Saturday: Granville, Barfleur, St-Vaast-la-Hougue, Barneville-Cartaret
Sunday: Barfleur

Ille-et-Vilaine
(coastal & waterway)
Monday: Redon, St. Briac-sur-Mer
Tuesday: Hédé, Rennes, Saint-Servan
Wednesday: Dinard, Rennes, Paramé, Tinteniac
Thursday: Guipry, Rennes
Friday: Rennes, St. Malo, St. Servan
Saturday: La Bouexiere, Paramé, Rennes, Dinard
Sunday: Betton, Cancale, le Richardais, Saint-Lunaire

Côtes d'Armor
Monday: Pontrieux, Saint-Cast-le-Guildo, Saint-Quay-Portrieux, Trégastel
Tuesday: Lancieux, Paimpol, Pléneuf, Trébeurden

Wednesday: Ile-Grande, Saint-Brieuc, Tréguier
Thursday: Binic, Dinan, Lannion
Friday: Lézardrieux, Perros-Guirec, La Roche-Derrien, Saint-Cast-le-Guildo, Saint-Quay-Portrieux, Saint-Jacut-de-la-Mer, Val André
Saturday: Erquy, Saint-Brieuc
Sunday: Nil

Finistère
Monday: Concarneau, Douarnenez, Ile Tudy
Tuesday: Le Conquet, Guilvinic, Loctudy, Pont Aven
Wednesday: Audierne, Lannillis, Morlaix, Roscoff
Thursday: Carentac, Chateaulin, Pont l'Abbé
Friday: Brignogan Plage, Concarneau, Douarnenez, Quimperlé, Saint Guénolé
Saturday: Audierne, Tréboul, Morlaix, Quimper
Sunday: Daoulas, Forêt Fouesnant

Calvados
Monday: Nil
Tuesday: Caen, Courseulles, Deauville, Grandcamp-Maisy, Ouistreham,
Wednesday: Cabourg, Caen, Isigny, Trouville

Thursday: Caen, Houlgate
Friday: Caen, Courseulles, Deauville, Ouistreham
Saturday: Caen, Dives-sur-Mer, Grandcamp-Maisy, Honfleur, Isigny
Sunday: Cabourg, Caen, Port-en-Bessin, Trouville

Seine Maritime
(including tidal Seine)
Monday: Nil
Tuesday: Duclair
Wednesday: Nil
Thursday: Etretat
Friday: St Valéry-en-Caux, Eu
Saturday: le Trait, Caudebec-en-Caux, Fécamp, Le Tréport
Sunday: Harfleur

Somme
Monday: Mers-les-Bains, Quend-Plage
Tuesday: Cayeux-sur-Mer, Le Crotoy, Fort Mahon
Wednesday: Ault-Onival
Thursday: Mers-les-Bains, Quend-Plage
Friday: Cayeux-sur-Mer, Le Crotoy, Fort Mahon
Saturday: Ault-Onival
Sunday: Cayeux-sur-Mer, Saint Valéry-sur-Somme

Nord-Pas de Calais
Monday: Grand-Fort-Philippe, Malo-Les-Bains, Le Touquet
Tuesday: Etaples, Berck-sur-Mer
Wednesday: Dunkerque, Boulogne-sur-Mer

Thursday: Le Touquet, Bray-Dunes
Friday: Gravelines, Berck-sur-Mer, Etaples
Saturday: Le Touquet, Boulogne-sur-Mer, Dunkerque
Sunday: Berck-sur-Mer

Customs (Douanes)

From 1st January 1993, fiscal frontiers between Member States of the EC were removed, allowing boat owners to move VAT-paid yachts freely between Member States without imposition of further tax. The 'six-month rule' which operated prior to 1st January 1993, allowed boats to be temporarily imported into France which made it possible for a UK yacht to take up residence in France with a limit of six months usage over any one year.

The owner of a VAT-paid boat can now, therefore, move the vessel anywhere within the EC without imposition of further tax and with no restrictions about length of stay.

Bonded stores

Perhaps we have the ferry companies to thank for bonded stores still being available to yachts 'visiting' France. After some highly successful lobbying, the cross-channel ferry operators will continue to sell duty-frees until 1999. Bonded stores for yachts will continue to be available and it is likely that the concession will be extended to 1997.

Ownership of a yacht based in French waters

For several years, the French authorities have applied legislation to protect their own domestic charter business. The skipper of a yacht based in French waters must be the owner (as indicated on the Certificate of Registry or Small Ships Register). This means that the boat owner cannot invite a friend to skipper the boat, unless this is a close member of the family. One way round this is to sell a nominal share in the boat and have the buyer's name added as joint-owner on the ship's papers. If there are more than two names on the Registry document, only the first two names are acceptable to the French authorities as Skipper. (The author's boat is owned by four members of the same family, and all are included on the Small Ship's Register; this has on a couple of occasions resulted in a complicated explanation of who is who on the boat!).

VAT/TVA

The application of VAT (or TVA in France) is complicated because there is no standard rate of VAT within the EC (currently UK VAT is 17.5% against a TVA in France of 18.6%). At the time of publication, some progress has been made on the VAT situation, but the EC guidelines relate only to new boats.

For new boats, larger than 7.5m, payment of tax will be levied in the country where the boat is to be kept. If a boat is built in the UK but destined for a permanent mooring in France, the UK Customs will make an allowance for trials in the UK, during which time no VAT will be levied. Immediately the boat takes up permanent residence in France the Douanes will require payment of TVA. On new boats under 7.5m, tax will be payable in the country of origin.

This leaves a vast grey area relating to tax on existing boats. Will it be possible to obtain from the UK Customs a Certificate which will be acceptable in other EC countries as proof that some form of tax has been paid (or that the UK Customs are satisfied that the boat owner has not deliberately avoided paying some form of tax on the boat)?

A large proportion of boat owners will have no evidence that VAT has been paid on the boat somewhere along the line if there have been several owners. There may well be some form of moratorium for these boat owners and those who own boats built before the introduction of VAT or Purchase Tax.

HM Customs and Excise have been inundated with enquiries from boat owners about VAT treatment of boats in EC waters. The following is part of a Customs and Excise press release, issued in the run up to 1st January 1993:

'The EC Commission has assured boat owners in an answer in the European Parliament that, where pleasure craft are kept in a Member State under the temporary importation rules deriving from Directive 83/182/EEC and on which VAT has already been paid, it confirms that there will be no obligation to pay VAT again after 31 December 1992

The government believes that no payment of VAT should be required on boats supplied in the UK before 1 April 1973 (when UK VAT started), or on boats imported into the UK on a duty paid basis before the date (including boats imported under the charge of residence concession).

Boats that remained in the UK for at least six months from the date of supply from new (i.e. not purchased under the Sailaway Boat Scheme or by a VAT registered person or company which reclaimed VAT as input tax) are likely to be VAT paid. Boat owners and potential buyers of boats without original documentation showing payment of VAT are advised to obtain as much information and documentation about VAT status of the vessel as possible. In the absence of the initial invoice or an import entry showing VAT payment, documents such as ships logs, records of surveys, *berthing records, accident reports, repair or overhaul records, correspondence with previous owners, manufacturer's details, etc. might help to establish whether or not a vessel is, or is likely to have been, VAT paid in the EC. The British Marine Industries Federation, through its membership, will try to assist any owners who have particular proof of payment problems.*

Customs recognise that the present (mid-1992) uncertainty may cause problems for boat owners or potential owners and they will issue firm information as soon as it becomes available.

Such information will, no doubt, also be published in the yachting magazines.

Météo

When in France, it makes sense not to rely exclusively on the BBC for shipping forecasts. There are no problems in receiving BBC Radio 4 on 198kHz/1515m, but there can be significant differences in what the weather will do on the English side of the Channel compared with the French side. The shipping forecast area Wight, for example, covers virtually the same area as the French *Météo Zone Manche East*; introduce 'locally' into the forecast for this area, and you can have a *jolie brise* off the Isle of Wight and a *vent frais* off Cherbourg.

The French forecast pinned up outside the harbour master's office can be studied at leisure, and anyone can at least read the forecast direction and strength of the wind. For the uninitiated, the *météo* on the French radio can be more difficult to follow. If listened to regularly, the same words occur over and over again. The French forecast is more descriptive compared with the English, with the use of words like *belle* and *énorme* to describe the sea-state, *jolie brise* and *violente tempête* relate to the wind strength.

Back in the UK, a good way for the boat owner to become familiar with the French forecast is, in the comfort of the armchair, to tune the domestic radio to the French National Radio (*France-Inter*) on 162kHz/1829m which covers all the French sea areas . These shipping forecasts are daily at 0645 and 2005 (local times). This can therefore be picked up in the UK at 0545 and 1905.

As in the UK, there are several different sources for shipping/weather forecasts:-
(all times are local)

National radio (LW)
France-Inter/Radio France 162kHz/1829m all Zones 0645, 2005

Local Radio (FM)
Radio-France Normandie Rouen between 0700 and 0800: 102.2 (Dieppe); 96.3 (Fécamp); 95.1 (Le Havre)
Radio-France Normandie Caen 0830: 102.2 (Le Havre); 102.6 (Caen)
Radio-France Cherbourg 0725,1830: 100.7 (Cherbourg); 99.8 (La Hague)
Radio-France Armorique 0755, 1255, 1855: 103.1 (Côtes-d'Armor and Ille-et-Vilaine; 101.3 (Vannes)

Radio Bretagne Ouest 0700,0740,0959,1800: 96.9 (Paimpol); 96.8 (Quimperle); 96.6 (Concarneau); 103.3 (Lorient); 93.0 (Quimper and Brest)

Telephone -*Minitel*
(recorded message) 36.15.08 followed by Départemental Number: 59 – Nord / 62 – Pas-de-Calais / 80 – Somme / 76 – Seine-Maritime /14 – Calvados / 50 – Manche / 35 – Ille-et-Vilaine / 22 – Côtes-d'Armor / 29 – Finistère

Telephone numbers of coastal stations *météorologiques*
Dunkerque   28 66 45 25 / Boulogne   21 31 52 23 /
Le Touquet   21 05 13 55 / Le Havre   35 42 21 06 /
Caen   31 26 68 11 / Cherbourg   33 22 91 77 / Dinard   99 46 10 46 /
St-Brieuc   96 94 94 09 / Brest   98 84 60 64 /
Quimper   98 94 03 43 / Lorient   97 64 34 86 /
Vannes   97 42 48 82 / Nantes   40 84 80 19

VHF
C.R.O.S.S. (coastguards/traffic control) VHF – following announcement on Ch 16.

C.R.O.S.S. Griz-Nez (traffic control Dover Straits) Hourly H+10 on Ch 11 in French and English
C.R.O.S.S. Jobourg (traffic control Cherbourg peninsula) Every half-hour H+20 and H+50 on Ch 11 in French and English; Ch 13 Granville, Barfleur, Ver-sur-Mer, Antifer
C.R.O.S.S. Corsen (traffic control Ouessant/Ushant) Granville to Penmarch Ch 13. 0800, 1515, 1915 (Fréhel); 0930, 1630, 1930 (Batz); 0900, 1600, 1900 (Sein)
C.R.O.S.S. Corsen (traffic control Ouessant/Ushant) Manche-Ouest, Ouest Bretagne, Nordd-Gascogne Ch11 in French and English every 3 hours (0150-2250); Ouissant/Ushant every 30 mins (H+10 and H+40)

France Telecom
(VHF at 0733 and 1233 following announcement on Ch 16).
Dunkerque – Cherbourg
Boulogne Radio FFB: Dunkerque Ch 61 / Calais Ch87 / Boulogne Ch23
Rouen TKY:Dieppe Ch 02 / Le Havre Ch 82 / Port-en-Bessin Ch 03 / Cherbourg Ch 27
St-Malo – St Nazaire
Le Conquet Radio: Saint-Malo Ch 02
FFU: Paimpol Ch 84 / Plougasnou Ch 81 / Le Conquet Ch 26 / Ouessant Ch 82 / Pont-L'Abbé Ch 86
St Nazaire Radio: Belle Ile Ch 87

Emergency Hospital/Dental Treatment in France

(abridged version of *'Health Advice for Travellers'* T4 March 1992 reproduced with kind permission of HMSO)

'Before travelling abroad, complete Forms CM1 and E111. Both are available from Post Offices. Hand both forms back to the Post Office who will retain CM1, handing back authorised E111 if you are eligible (resident of UK). A photocopy of this document is recommended. The E111 can cover traveller and dependants.

With the completed Form E111, a visitor to France (and other EC Countries) can receive subsidised medical or dental treatment. This only relates to urgent treatment for accidents or unexpected illness.If you intend getting medical treatment while you are abroad, form E111 will not cover the costs.

If Form E111 is not used, it is valid indefinitely. If a claim is made using Form E111, then an application for a new one must be made before the next trip to France.'

Visiting France

Where to get information/refunds
Outside Paris: local sickness insurance offices *(Caisses Primaires d'Assurance-Maladie)*.
Paris: *Caisse Primaire d'Assurance-Maladie de Paris*, Service des Relations Internationales, 173-175 rue de Bercy, 75586 Paris Cedex 12. Tel 43 46 12 53

Medical and dental treatment
Make sure the doctor or dentist you consult is *'conventionne'*: this means they work with the French sickness insurance scheme. After treatment make sure the doctor or dentist gives you the signed statement of treatment given *('feuille de soins')*. You cannot claim a refund without it. You will be charged for treatment and prescribed medicines, and the doctor, dentist or chemist will write the amount on the *'feuille de soins'*.

The chemist will hand back the prescription. Attach it to the *'feuille de soins'*. The medicine containers have detachable stamps *('vignettes')* which show the name and cost of the medicine. Stick the *'vignettes'* in the appropriate space on the *'feuille de soins'* and sign and date the form at the end. Send your application for a refund (the *'feuille de soins'* and prescription and form E111) to the local sickness insurance office for the area while your are still in France. The refund will be sent on to your home address later, but before sending the money order, the office will send you a statement itemising the amount to be refunded. This may take some time.

You will be refunded about 75% of the medical or dental standard fee and between 40% and 70% of the cost of most prescribed medicines (the cost of common remedies or items such as bandages are refunded at a lower rate – about 40%, and the costs of medicines marked with the *'vignette'* ▲ are not recoverable).

Hospital treatment

You must pay for outpatient treatment and then claim a refund from the local sickness insurance office (as explained for medical treatment).If you need in-patient hospital treatment, the doctor you have consulted or the hospital doctor will issue you with a certificate *('attestation')*. The hospital will probably send the 'Notice of admission – Acceptance of responsibility' form *('Avis d' admission-prise en charge')* to the local sickness insurance office with your form E111 attached. If not, you will have to send it yourself.If you get treatment in an approved hospital, the sickness insurance office will pay its share (80% or more) direct to the hospital. You have to pay the balance. You may also have to pay the fixed daily hospital charge *('forfait journalier')*.

If you could not get a refund abroad, write explaining why to: Department of Social Security, Overseas Branch (MED), Newcastle upon Tyne, NE98 1YX. Send your E111, original bills, prescriptions and receipts. Fill in and sign page 1 of the *'feuille de soins'*. Attach to this the *'vignettes'* (stamps supplied with prescribed medicine).

Private medical care

If you have private medical insurance, check that this adequately covers you while you are in France. Some private insurance does not include supply of drugs.

Motoring

The E111 may not cover your medical/hospital expenses if you are driving and are involved in a car accident. Check your motor insurance.

Addresses and Telephone Numbers

Brittany Canals (information)
Equipement, Ille et Vilaine,1 Avenue du Mail, 35000 Rennes
tel 99 59 2060   tel 99 59 11 12 (recorded information)
Charts & Brittany Canals Guides
Kelvin Hughes Ltd.,Charts & Maritime Supplies,145 Minories,London
EC3N 1NH   tel 071 709 9076
Stanfords, 12 – 14 Long Acre, London WC2E 9LP   tel 071 836 1321
Customs
Centre de Renseignements Douaniers, 182 rue St-Honore, 75001 Paris
tel (1) 42 60 35 90
Emergency tel nos in France
Ambulance 15 / Police   17 / Fire   18
Ferry Operators
Brittany Ferries – Plymouth (0752) 221321/ – Portsmouth (0705)
827701/ – Poole (0202) 666466
Hoverspeed – Dover (0304) 240101 / – Calais 21 96 67 10 /
– Boulogne 21 30 27 26
P&O European – London (081) 575 8555 / – Dover (0304) 203388 / –
Portsmouth (0705) 772244 / – Calais 21 46 10 10 /
– Boulogne 21 31 78 00 / – Le Havre 35 21 36 50 /
– Cherbourg 33 44 20 13
Sally Ferries – Ramsgate (0843) 595522 / – London (081) 858 1127 / –
Dunkerque 28 21 43 44
Sealink Stena (central res.) – (0233) 647047 / – Dover (0304) 240028 /
– Newhaven (0273) 512266 / Southampton(0703) 233973
Truckline (Brittany Ferries) Poole (0202) 666466
RYA, RYA House, Romsey Road, Eastleigh, Hampshire, SO5 4YA
tel   0703 629962
Search and Rescue
CROSS-GRIS NEZ (Straits of Dover to Le Havre)   tel 21 87 40 40
CROSS-MANCHE (Cherbourg,Le Havre,Channel Is) tel   33 52 78 23
CROSS-CORSEN (Ushant,Channel Is,Bay of Biscay) tel   98 89 31 31
CROS-ETEL (North Bay of Biscay) tel   97 55 35 35
Weather telephone numbers – see Météo page 136

Yacht harbours at Ferry Terminals

Dunkerque:Yacht Club Mer du Nord (YCMN), Qaie des Monitors, 59140, Dunkerque

tel Capitainerie	28 66 79 90
(Y.C.M.N.)	28 66 17 84

Calais: Port de Plaisance, Bassin Ouest, Calais 62100

tel Port de Plaisance	21 34 55 23
Yacht Club de Calais (YCC)	21 97 02 34

Boulogne:Bureau de Port de Plaisance, quai Chanzy, 62200, Boulogne

tel Port de Plaisance	21 31 70 01
Yacht-Club Boulonnais (YCB)	21 31 80 67

Dieppe: Cercle de Voile de Dieppe, (C.V.D.), Quai de la Poissonnerie, B.P. 1020, 76205, Dieppe

tel Capitainerie du Port de Plaisance	35 84 32 99
(C.V.D.)	35 84 22 29

Le Havre: Le Havre Plaisance, Boulevard Clemenceau, 76600, Le Havre

tel Port de Plaisance	35 22 72 72
Société des Régates du Havre (SRH)	35 42 41 21

Ouistreham: Capitainerie de Ouistreham, Quai Georges-Thieiérry, Bassin de Plaisance, 14150, Ouistreham

tel Capitainerie	31 97 14 43
Société des Régates de Caen-Ouistreham (SRCO)	31 97 13 05

Cherbourg: Capitainerie, Port Chantereyne, 50100, Cherbourg

tel Capitainerie	33 53 75 16
Yacht Club de Cherbourg	33 53 02 83

St Malo: Capitainerie, Port Vauban, 35400, St Malo

tel Capitainerie	99 56 51 91
SN Baie de Saint-Malo	99 40 84 42

Morlaix: Capitainerie, Port de Plaisance, Quai de Treguier, 29600, Morlaix

tel Capitainerie	98 62 13 14
Yacht-Club de Morlaix (YCM)	98 88 25 85

Brest: Capitainerie, Bureau du Port de Plaisance du Moulin-Blanc, 29200, Brest

tel Port de Plaisance	98 02 20 02

Index